THE EASY FORTIES FAKE BOOK

Melody, Lyrics and Simplified Chords

100 Songs in  '40s the Key of "C"

THE EASY FORTIES FAKE BOOK

ISBN 0-634-08823-8

HAL•LEONARD®
CORPORATION
7777 W. BLUEMOUND RD. P.O. BOX 13819 MILWAUKEE, WI 53213

Visit Hal Leonard Online at
www.halleonard.com

THE EASY FORTIES FAKE BOOK

CONTENTS

INTRODUCTION

What Is a Fake Book?

A fake book has one-line music notation consisting of melody, lyrics and chord symbols. This lead sheet format is a "musical shorthand" which is an invaluable resource for all musicians—hobbyists to professionals.

Here's how *The Easy Forties Fake Book* differs from most standard fake books:

- All songs are in the key of C.

- Many of the melodies have been simplified.

- Only five basic chord types are used—major, minor, seventh, diminished and augmented.

- The music notation is larger for ease of reading.

In the event that you haven't used chord symbols to create accompaniment, or your experience is limited, a chord speller chart is included at the back of the book to help you get started.

Have fun!

AC-CENT-TCHU-ATE THE POSITIVE
from the Motion Picture HERE COME THE WAVES

Lyric by JOHNNY MERCER
Music by HAROLD ARLEN

ACROSS THE ALLEY FROM THE ALAMO

Words and M
JOE GR

Easy Swing

A - cross the al - ley from the al - a - mo, ___ lived a pin - to po - ny and

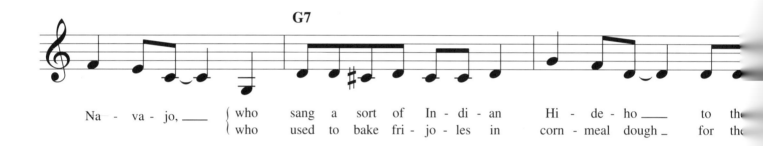

Na - va - jo, ___ { who sang a sort of In - di - an Hi - de - ho ___ to the
{ who used to bake fri - jo - les in corn - meal dough _ for the

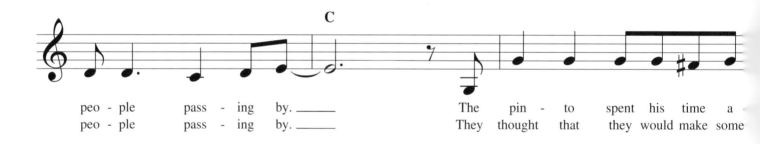

peo - ple pass - ing by. _____ The pin - to spent his time a
peo - ple pass - ing by. _____ They thought that they would make some

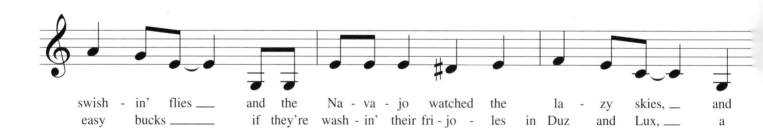

swish - in' flies ___ and the Na - va - jo watched the la - zy skies, ___ and
easy bucks _____ if they're wash - in' their fri - jo - les in Duz and Lux, ___ a

ver - y rare - ly did they ever rest their eyes _____ on the
pair of ver - y con - sci - en - tious clucks ___ to the

ALL OR NOTHING AT ALL

Words by JACK LAWR
Music by ARTHUR AL

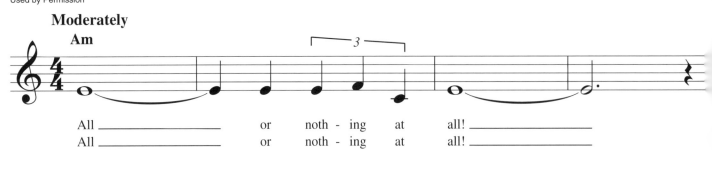

All _____ or noth - ing at all! _____
All _____ or noth - ing at all! _____

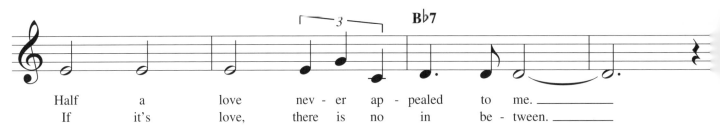

Half a love nev - er ap - pealed to me. _____
If it's love, there is no in be - tween. _____

If your heart nev - er could yield to me, _____ then } I'd
Why be - gin, then cry for some-thing that might have been? _____ No, }

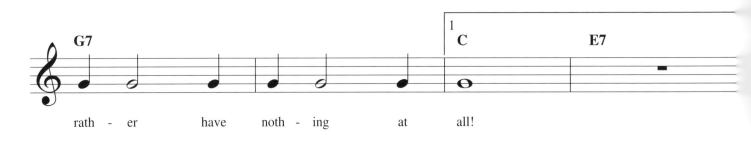

rath - er have noth - ing at all!

all. _____ But, please, don't bring your lips so close to my

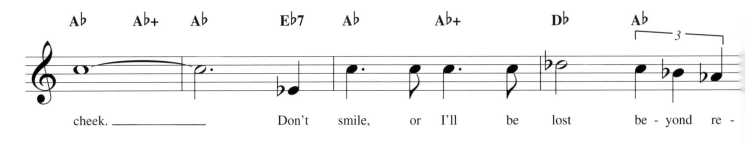

cheek. _____ Don't smile, or I'll be lost be - yond re -

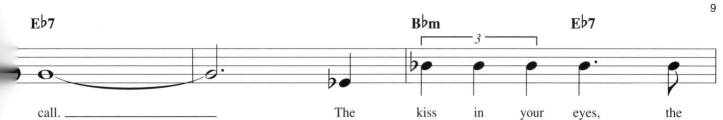

call. _____ The kiss in your eyes, the

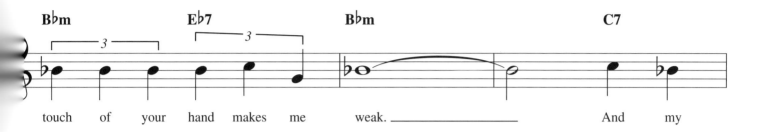

touch of your hand makes me weak. _____ And my

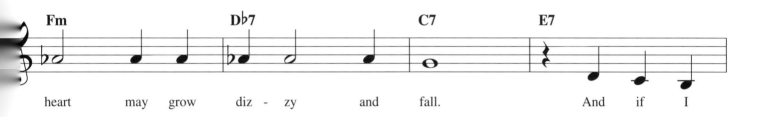

heart may grow diz - zy and fall. And if I

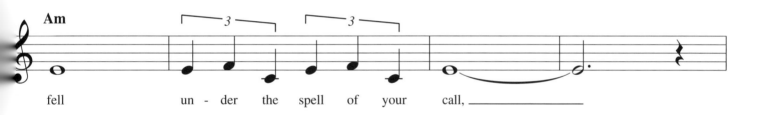

fell un - der the spell of your call, _____

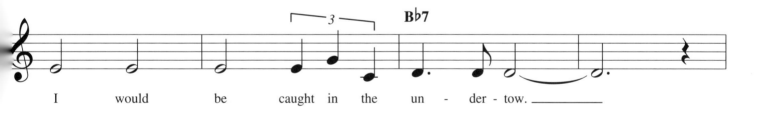

I would be caught in the un - der - tow. _____

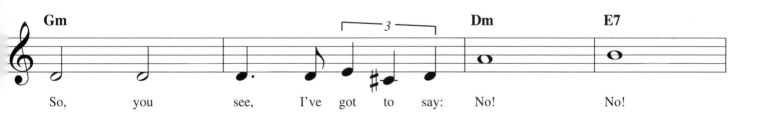

So, you see, I've got to say: No! No!

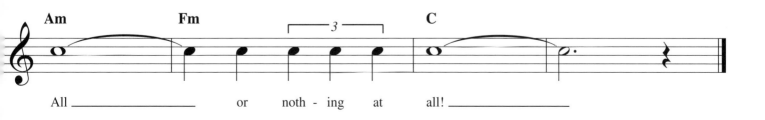

All _____ or noth - ing at all! _____

AMOR
(Amor, Amor, Amor)

Music by GABRIEL
Spanish Words by RICARDO LOPEZ MEN
English Words by NORMAN NE

THE ANNIVERSARY WALTZ

Words and Music by AL D
and DAVE FRAN

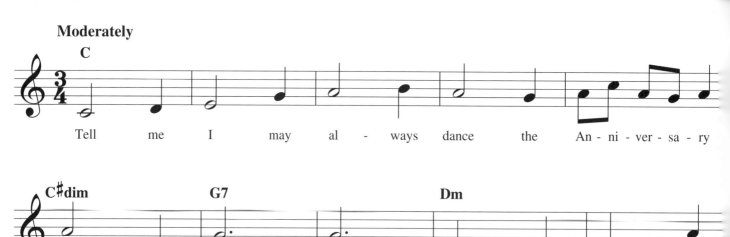

Tell me I may al - ways dance the An - ni - ver - sa - ry

Waltz with you. _____ Tell me this is

real ro - mance, an an - ni - ver - sa - ry dream come true. _____

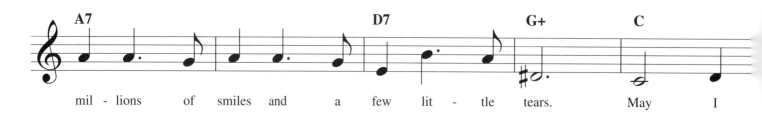

_____ Let this be the an - them to our fu - ture years, to

mil - lions of smiles and a few lit - tle tears. May I

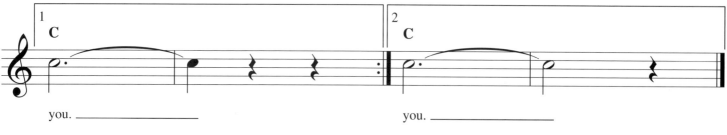

al - ways lis - ten to the An - ni - ver - sa - ry Waltz with

you. _____   you. _____

BE CAREFUL, IT'S MY HEART
from HOLIDAY INN

Words and Music by
IRVING BERLIN

AREN'T YOU GLAD YOU'RE YOU

Words by JOHNNY BU
Music by JIMMY VAN HEU

Moderately

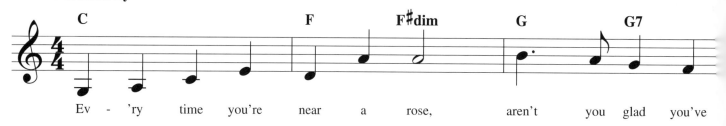

Ev - 'ry time you're near a rose, aren't you glad you've

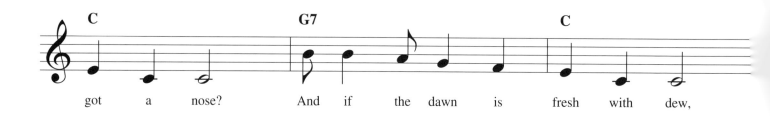

got a nose? And if the dawn is fresh with dew,

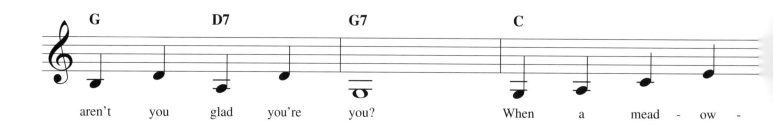

aren't you glad you're you? When a mead - ow -

lark ap - pears, aren't you glad you've got two ears?

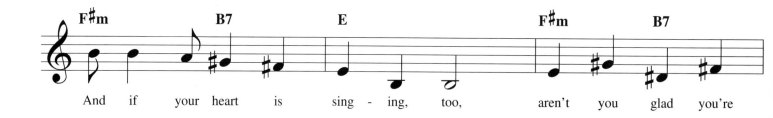

And if your heart is sing - ing, too, aren't you glad you're

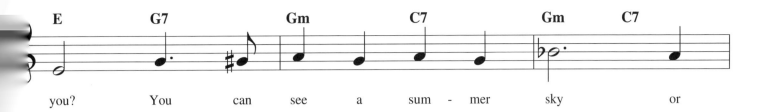

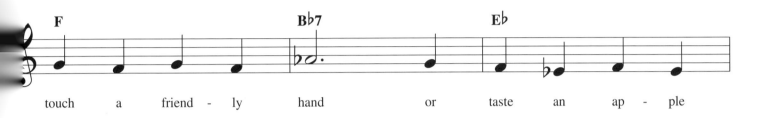

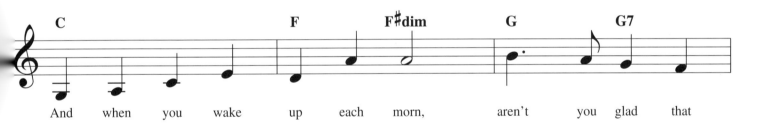

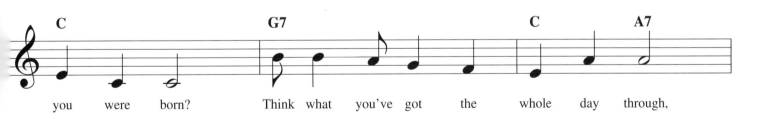

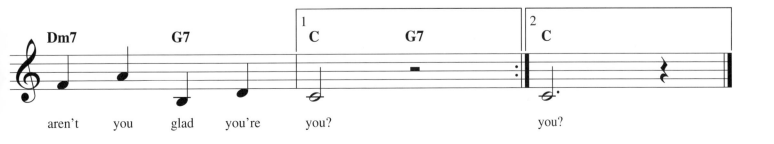

BÉSAME MUCHO
(Kiss Me Much)

Music and Spanish Words by CONSUELO VELAZQ
English Words by SUNNY SKY

Moderate Latin

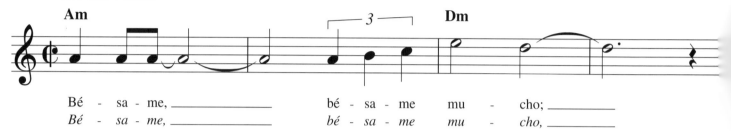

Bé - sa - me, _____ bé - sa - me mu - cho; _____
Bé - sa - me, _____ bé - sa - me mu - cho, _____

Each time I cling to your kiss I hear mu - sic di - vine; _____
co - mo si fue - ra es - ta no - che la úl - ti - ma vez; _____

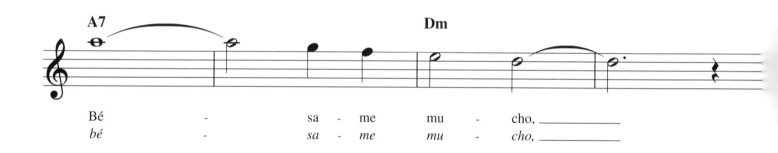

Bé - sa - me mu - cho, _____
bé - sa - me mu - cho, _____

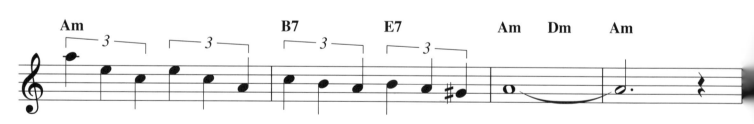

Hold me, my dar - ling, and say that you'll al - ways be mine. _____
que ten - go mie - do per - der - te, per - der - te o - tra vez. _____

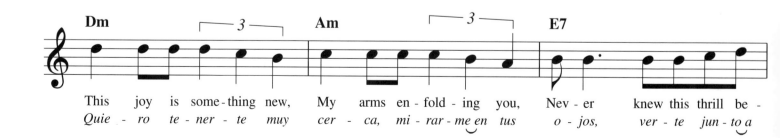

This joy is some - thing new, My arms en - fold - ing you, Nev - er knew this thrill be -
Quie - ro te - ner - te muy cer - ca, mi - rar - me en tus o - jos, ver - te jun - to a

BEWITCHED

from PAL JOEY

Words by LORENZ H
Music by RICHARD ROD

Slowly

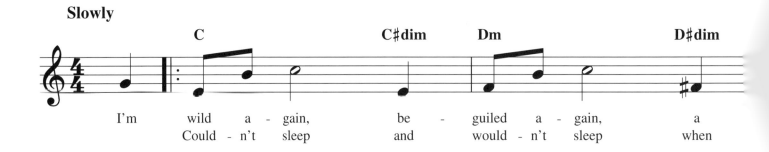

I'm wild a - gain, be - guiled a - gain, a
Could - n't sleep and would - n't sleep when

sim - per - ing, whim - per - ing child a - gain, be -
love came and told me I should - n't sleep, be -

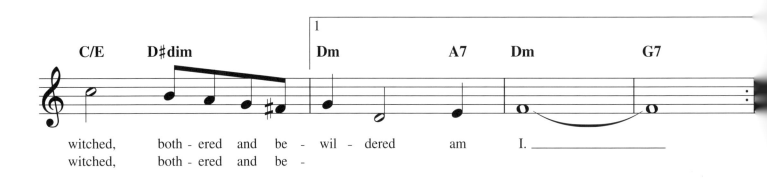

witched, both - ered and be - wil - dered am I.
witched, both - ered and be -

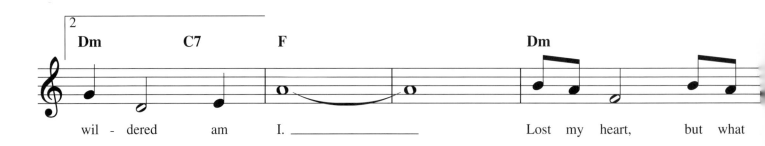

wil - dered am I.   Lost my heart, but what

19

of it.   He is cold,   I a - gree.

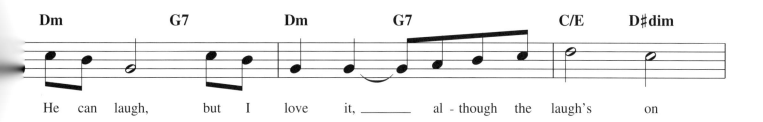

He can laugh,   but I love it, _____ al - though the laugh's on

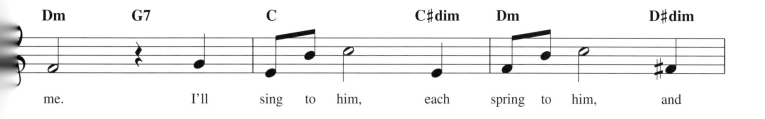

me.   I'll sing to him,   each spring to him,   and

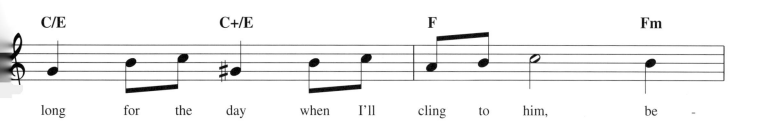

long   for the day   when I'll cling to him,   be -

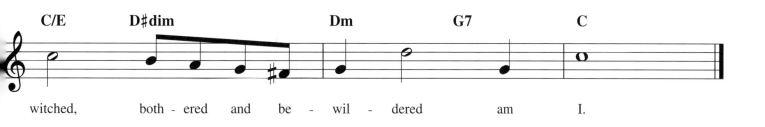

witched,   both - ered and be - wil - dered am I.

BIBBIDI-BOBBIDI-BOO
(The Magic Song)
from Walt Disney's CINDERELLA

Words by JERRY LIVINGS
Music by MACK DAVID and AL HOFF

Brightly

Sa - la - ga - doo - la men - chic - ka boo - la bib - bi - di - bob - bi - di - boo,

put 'em to - geth - er and what have you got bib - bi - di - bob - bi - di - boo.

Sa - la - ga - doo - la men - chic - ka boo - la bib - bi - di - bob - bi - di - boo,

it - 'll do mag - ic be - lieve it or not, bib - bi - di- bob - bi - di - boo. Sa - la - ga - doo - la means

men - chic - ka boo - le - roo, but the thing - a - ma - bob that does the job is

bib - bi - di - bob - bi - di - boo. Sa - la - ga - doo - la men - chic - ka boo - la

bib - bi - di - bob - bi - di - boo, put 'em to - geth - er and what have you got

DADDY'S LITTLE GIRL

Words and Music by BOBBY BURKE
and HORACE GERLACH

Moderately

You're the end of the rain - bow, my pot o' gold. You're

dad - dy's lit - tle girl to have and hold. A pre - cious

gem is what you are, you're mom - my's bright and

shin - ing star. You're the spir - it of Christ - mas, my star on the
You're the treas - ure I cher - ish, so spar - kling and

tree, you're the Eas - ter bun - ny to mom - my and me. You're
bright, you were touched by ho - ly and beau - ti - ful light, like

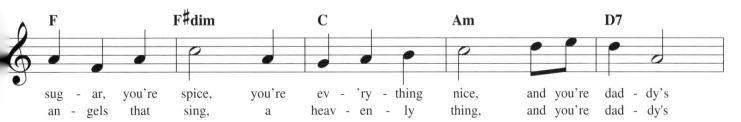

sug - ar, you're spice, you're ev - 'ry - thing nice, and you're dad - dy's
an - gels that sing, a heav - en - ly thing, and you're dad - dy's

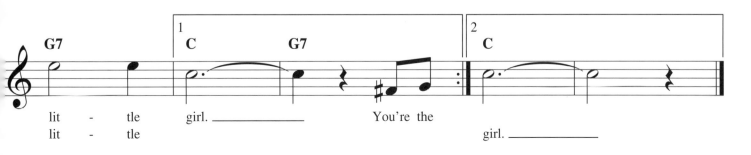

lit - tle girl. _____ You're the
lit - tle girl. _____

BOOGIE WOOGIE BUGLE BOY
from BUCK PRIVATES

Words and Music by DON
and HUGHIE PF

Medium Boogie Woogie

They made him blow a bu - gle for his Un - cle Sam, ___ it
puts the boys to sleep with "boo - gie" ev - 'ry night, ___ and

real - ly brought him down be - cause he could - n't jam. ___ The cap - tain
wakes them up the same way in the ear - ly bright. ___ They clap their

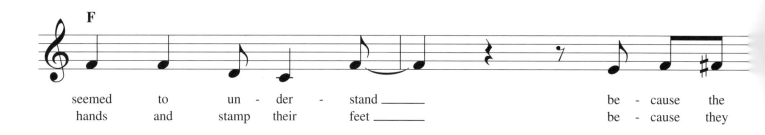

seemed to un - der - stand _____ be - cause the
hands and stamp their feet _____ be - cause they

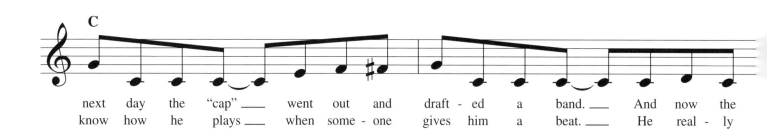

next day the "cap" ___ went out and draft - ed a band. ___ And now the
know how he plays ___ when some - one gives him a beat. ___ He real - ly

com - p'ny jumps } when he plays re - veil - le, he's the
breaks it up }

BOUQUET OF ROSES

Words and Music by STEVE NE—
and BOB HILL—

Moderately

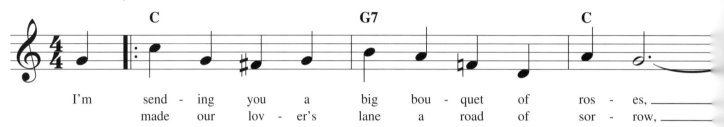

I'm send - ing you a big bou - quet of ros - es, ____
made our lov - er's lane a road of sor - row, ____

____ one for ev - 'ry time you broke my
____ till at last we had to say good -

heart. ____ And as the door of
bye. ____ You're leav - ing me to

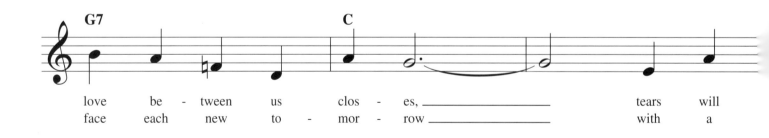

love be - tween us clos - es, ____ tears will
face each new to - mor - row ____ with a

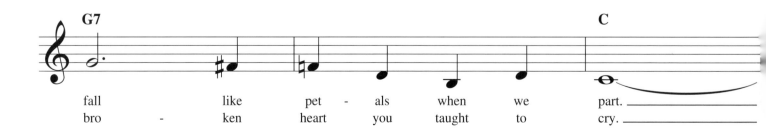

fall like pet - als when we part. ____
bro - ken heart you taught to cry. ____

I begged you to be dif - f'rent but you'll
I know that I should hate you af - ter

al - ways be un - true. I'm tir - ed of for -
all you've put me thru. But how can I be

giv - ing, now there's noth - ing left to do. }
bit - ter, when I'm still in love with you? }
So I'm

send - ing you a big bou - quet of ros - es, _____

_____ one for ev - 'ry time you broke my

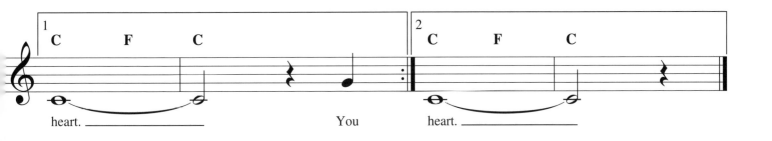

heart. _____ You
heart. _____

BUTTONS AND BOWS

from the Paramount Picture THE PALEFACE

Words and Music by JAY LIVINGS
and RAY EV

Lively

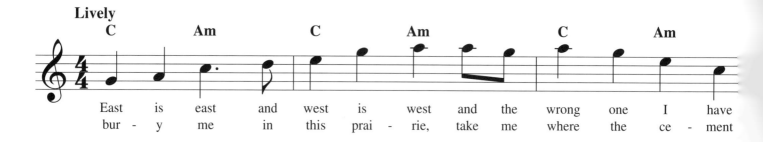

East is east and west is west and the wrong one I have
bur - y me in this prai - rie, take me where the ce - ment

chose.   Let's go where you'll keep on wear - in' those
grows.   Let's move down to some big town where they

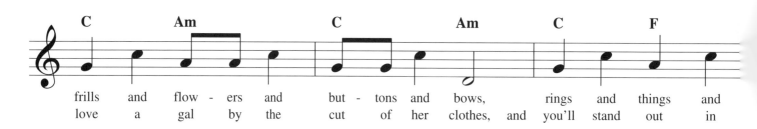

frills and flow - ers and but - tons and bows,   rings and things and
love a gal by the cut of her clothes, and you'll stand out in

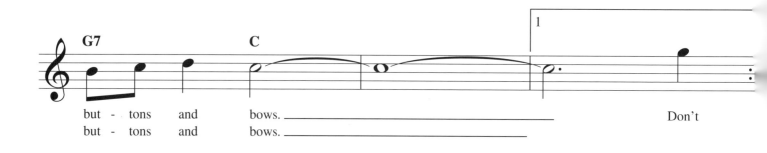

1.

but - tons and bows. _____   Don't
but - tons and bows. _____

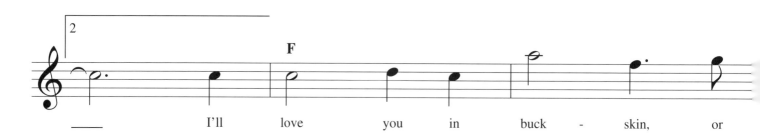

2.

_____ I'll love you in buck - skin, or

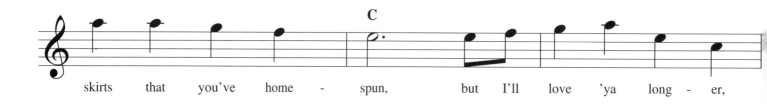

skirts that you've home - spun, but I'll love 'ya long - er,

27

CHI-BABA CHI-BABA
(My Bambino Go to Sleep)

Words and Music by MACK DA
AL HOFFMAN and JERRY LIVINGS

Slowly, with a lilt

Chi - ba - ba, chi - ba - ba, chi - wa - wa, en - ja - la - wa, cook - a - la goom - ba.   Chi

ba - ba, chi - ba - ba, chi - wa - wa, my bam - bi - no go to sleep.   Chi -

ba - ba, chi - ba - ba, chi - wa - wa, en - ja - la - wa, cook - a - la goom - ba.   Chi -

ba - ba, chi - ba - ba, chi - wa - wa my bam - bi - no go to sleep.

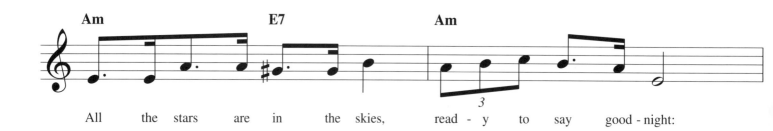

All   the   stars   are   in   the   skies,   read - y   to   say   good - night:

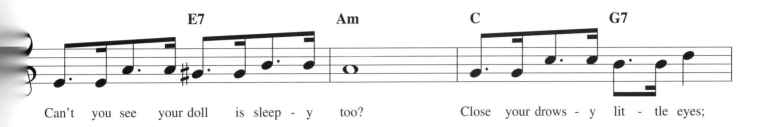

Can't you see your doll is sleep - y too? Close your drows - y lit - tle eyes;

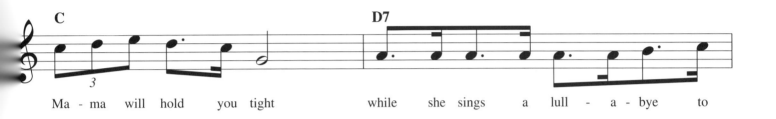

Ma - ma will hold you tight while she sings a lull - a - bye to

you. _____ Chi - ba - ba, chi - ba - ba, chi - wa - wa. en - ja -

la - wa, cook - a - la goom - ba. Chi - ba - ba, chi - ba - ba, chi - wa - wa my bam -

bi - no, go to sleep. Chi - bi - no, go to sleep.

COME RAIN OR COME SHINE
from ST. LOUIS WOMAN

Words by JOHNNY MER
Music by HAROLD AR

Slowly

I'm gon - na love you like no - bod - y's loved you come

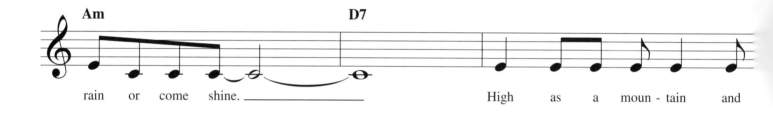

rain or come shine._____ High as a moun - tain and

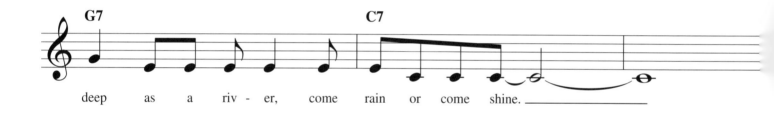

deep as a riv - er, come rain or come shine._____

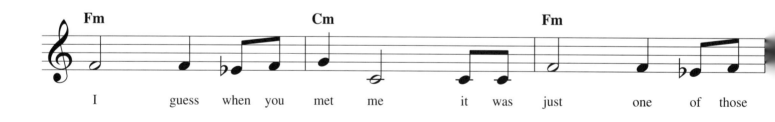

I guess when you met me it was just one of those

things. But don't ev - er bet me, 'cause I'm

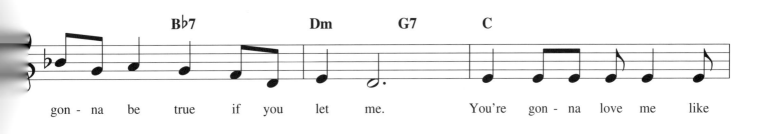

gon - na be true if you let me. You're gon - na love me like

no - bod - y's loved me come rain or come shine. _____

Hap - py to - geth - er, un - hap - py to - geth - er and

won't it be fine. _____ Days may be cloud - y or

sun - ny, we're in or we're out of the mon - ey. But

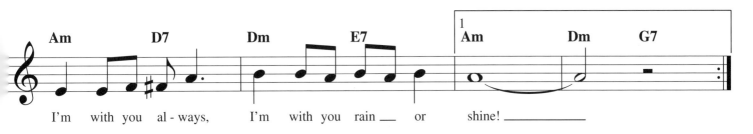

I'm with you al - ways, I'm with you rain __ or shine! _____

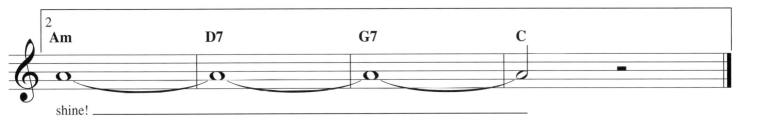

shine! _____

CRAZY HE CALLS ME

Words and Music by BOB RUS:
and CARL SIG

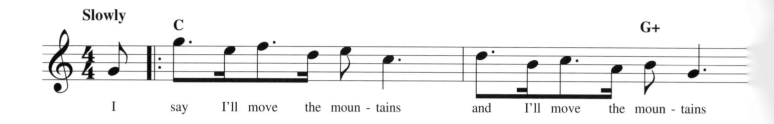

I say I'll move the moun-tains and I'll move the moun-tains

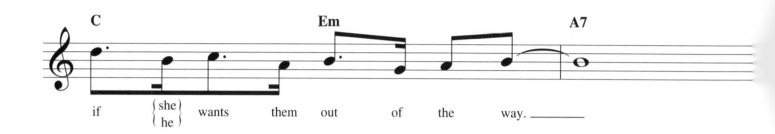

if {she}{he} wants them out of the way. _____

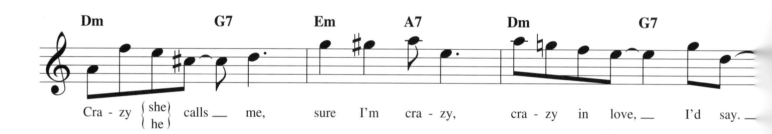

Cra-zy {she}{he} calls ___ me, sure I'm cra-zy, cra-zy in love, ___ I'd say. __

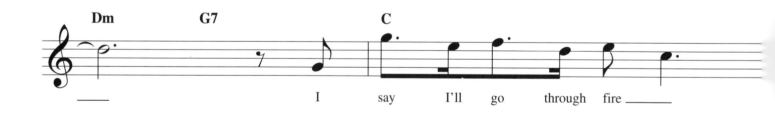

____ I say I'll go through fire _____

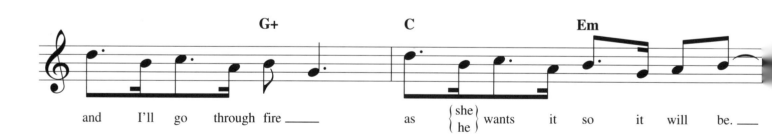

and I'll go through fire _____ as {she}{he} wants it so it will be.

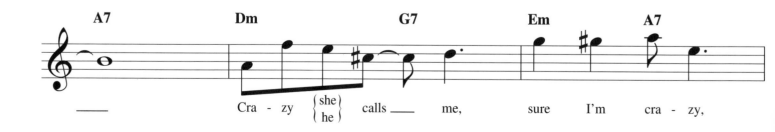

____ Cra-zy {she}{he} calls ___ me, sure I'm cra-zy,

DANCE WITH A DOLLY (WITH A HOLE IN HER STOCKIN')

Words and Music by TERRY SH
JIMMY EATON and MICKEY LEA

Medium Bounce

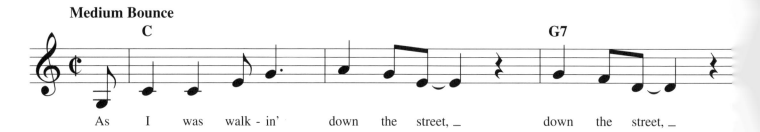

As I was walk-in' down the street, __ down the street, __

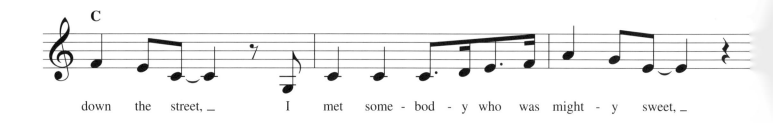

down the street, __ I met some-bod-y who was might-y sweet, __

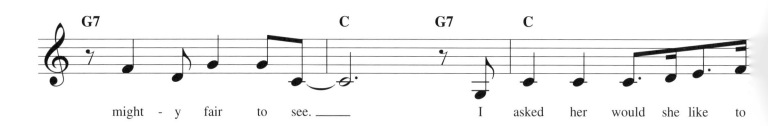

might-y fair to see. _____ I asked her would she like to

have a talk, ___ have a talk, ___ make some talk.

All the fel-lows stand-in' on the walk __ wish-in' they were me: ___

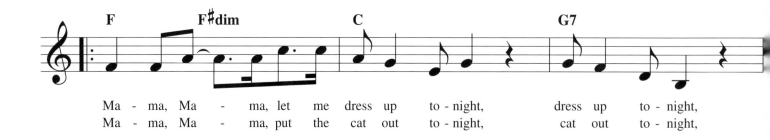

Ma-ma, Ma-ma, let me dress up to-night, dress up to-night,
Ma-ma, Ma-ma, put the cat out to-night, cat out to-night,

dress up to-night. I've got a se - cret, gon - na 'fess up to-night gon - na
cat out to-night. Worked all day, I'm gon - na scat out to-night and I

dance by the light of the moon. _____
won't be home un - til dawn. _____
Gon - na dance with a dol - ly with a

hole in her stock - in' while our knees keep a - knock - in' and our

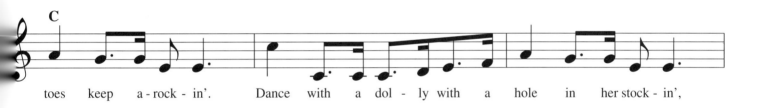

toes keep a - rock - in'. Dance with a dol - ly with a hole in her stock - in',

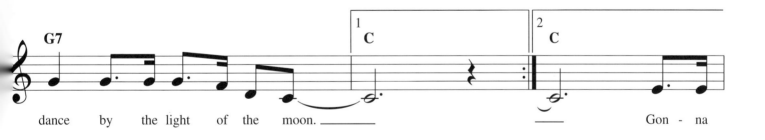

dance by the light of the moon. _____ _____ Gon - na

dance by the light of the moon. ___ Dance by the light of the moon, _

_____ by the light _____ of the moon. _____

DAY BY DAY

Theme from the Paramount Television Series DAY BY DAY

Words and Music by SAMMY C
AXEL STORDAHL and PAUL WE

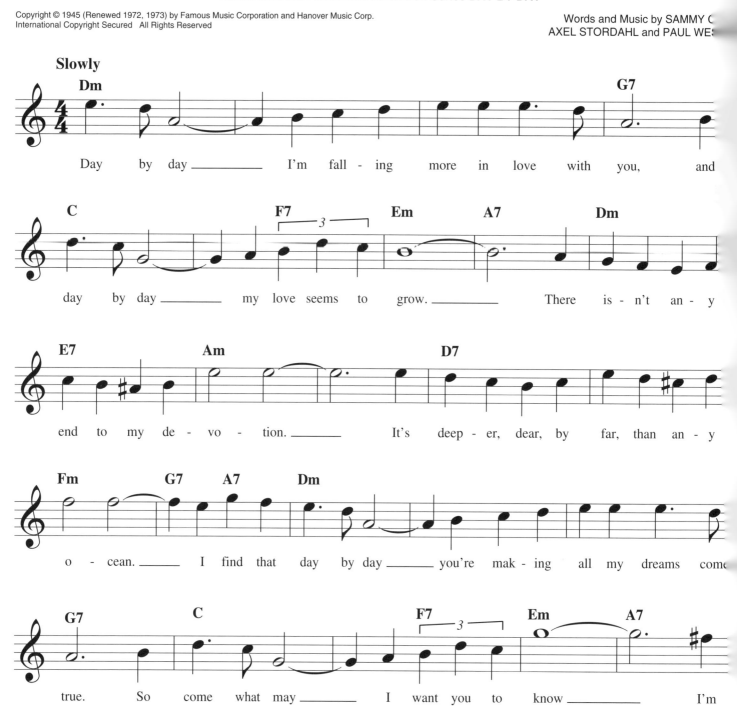

Day by day _____ I'm fall - ing more in love with you, and

day by day _____ my love seems to grow. _____ There is - n't an - y

end to my de - vo - tion. _____ It's deep - er, dear, by far, than an - y

o - cean. _____ I find that day by day _____ you're mak - ing all my dreams come

true. So come what may _____ I want you to know _____ I'm

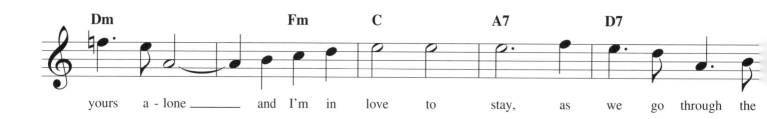

yours a - lone _____ and I'm in love to stay, as we go through the

years, day by day. _____   day. _____

DEARLY BELOVED
from YOU WERE NEVER LOVELIER

Music by JEROME KERN
Words by JOHNNY MERCER

Moderately

Dear - ly be - lov - ed how clear - ly I see. Some - where in

heav - en you were fash - ioned for me. An - gel eyes _____

knew you, _____ an - gel voic - es led me to you. _____

Noth - ing can stop me, fate gave me a sign. I know that

I'll be yours come show - er or shine. So I say _____

mere - ly, _____ Dear - ly be - lov - ed be mine. _____

DEEP IN THE HEART OF TEXAS

Words by JUNE HER
Music by DON SWAI

Lively

C

The stars at night are big and bright,
coy - otes wail a - long the bright trail,

deep in the heart of Tex - as. _____ { The
{ The

prair - ie sky is wide and high,
rab - bits rush a - round the high brush,
deep in the

G7

heart of Tex - as. _____ { The sage in
{ The cow - boys

bloom is like per - fume,
cry, "Ki - yip - pee - yi,"
deep in the heart of

G7

Tex - as. _____ { Re - minds me of the one I love,
{ The do - gies bawl, and bawl and bawl,

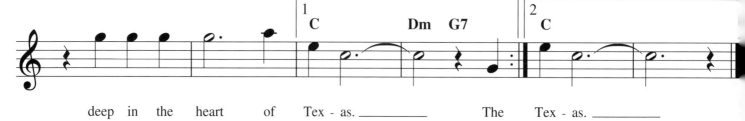

| 1 | | 2 |
| C | Dm G7 | C |

deep in the heart of Tex - as. _____   The Tex - as. _____

DOLORES
from the Paramount Picture LAS VEGAS NIGHTS

Words by FRANK LOESSER
Music by LOUIS ALTER

Moderately

How I love the kiss - es of Do - lo - res ay, ay, ay Do -
I would die to be with my Do - lo - res ay, ay, ay Do -

lo - res; not Ma - rie or Em - i - ly or Dor - is,
lo - res. I was made to ser - e - nade Do - lo - res,

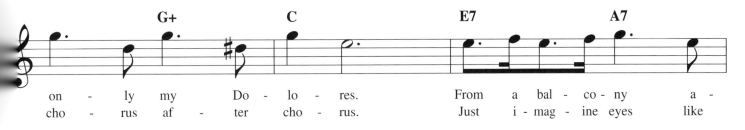

on - ly my Do - lo - res. From a bal - co - ny a -
cho - rus af - ter cho - rus. Just i - mag - ine eyes like

bove me, _____ she whis - pers "Love me," _____ and throws a rose.
moon - rise _____ a voice like mu - sic, _____ and lips like

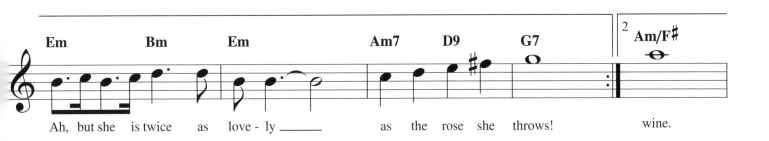

Ah, but she is twice as love - ly _____ as the rose she throws! wine.

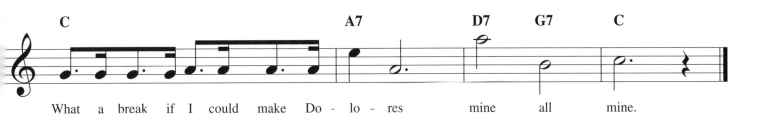

What a break if I could make Do - lo - res mine all mine.

DON'T GET AROUND MUCH ANYMORE

from SOPHISTICATED LADY

Words and Music by DUKE ELLING...
and BOB RUSS...

A DREAM IS A WISH YOUR HEART MAKES
from Walt Disney's CINDERELLA

Words and Music by MACK DAVID,
AL HOFFMAN and JERRY LIVINGSTON

Moderately

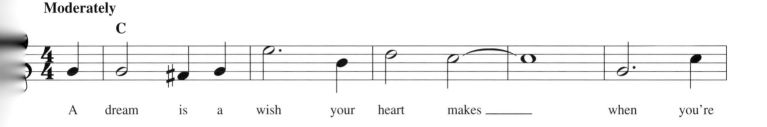

A dream is a wish your heart makes _____ when you're

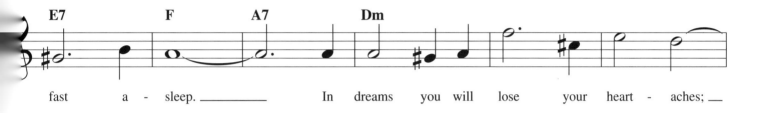

fast a - sleep. _____ In dreams you will lose your heart - aches; __

__ what - ev - er you wish for, you keep. Have faith in your

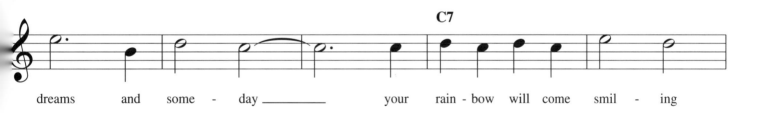

dreams and some - day _____ your rain - bow will come smil - ing

thru. _____ No mat - ter how your heart is griev - ing, if you keep on be -

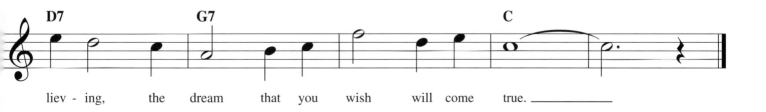

liev - ing, the dream that you wish will come true. _____

EARLY AUTUMN

Words by JOHNNY MER
Music by RALPH BURNS and WOODY HER

When an ear-ly au-tumn walks the land _____ and chills the breeze and
vil-ion in the rain _____ all shut-tered down. A

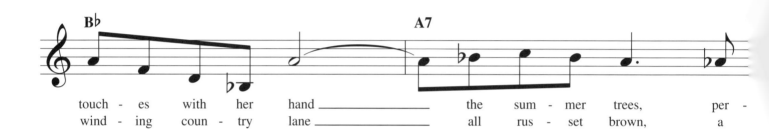

touch-es with her hand _____ the sum-mer trees, per-a
wind-ing coun-try lane _____ all rus-set brown, a

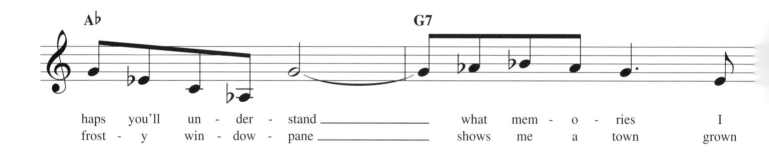

haps you'll un-der-stand _____ what mem-o-ries I
frost-y win-dow-pane _____ shows me a town grown

own. _____ There's a dance pa- lone - ly. _____

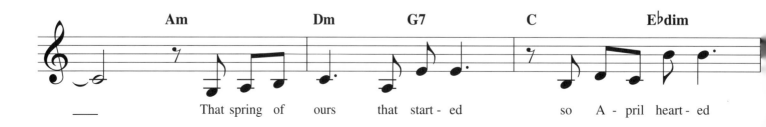

_____ That spring of ours that start-ed so A-pril heart-ed

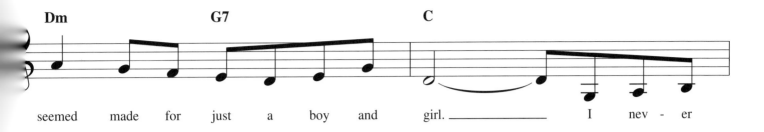

seemed made for just a boy and girl. _____ I nev - er

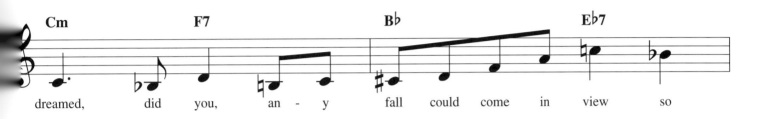

dreamed, did you, an - y fall could come in view so

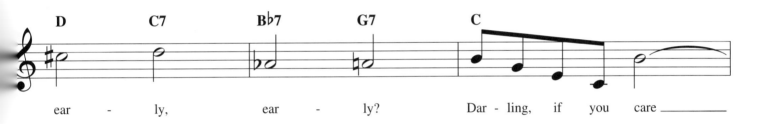

ear - ly, ear - ly? Dar - ling, if you care _____

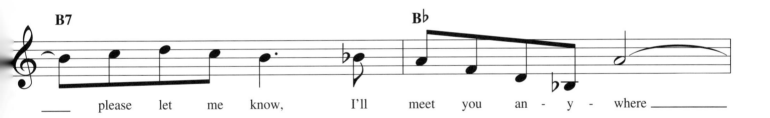

_____ please let me know, I'll meet you an - y - where _____

_____ I miss you so. Let's nev - er have to share _____

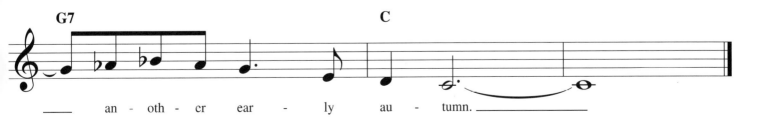

_____ an - oth - er ear - ly au - tumn. _____

EASY DOES IT

Words and Music by SY OL‌
and JIMMY YO‌

Moderately

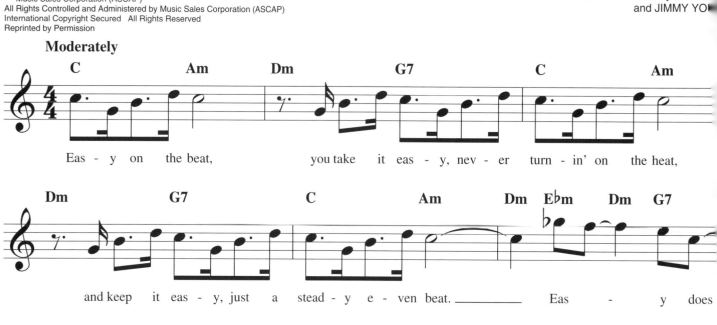

Eas - y on the beat, you take it eas - y, nev - er turn - in' on the heat,

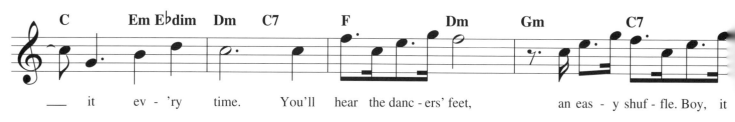

and keep it eas - y, just a stead - y e - ven beat._____ Eas - y does

___ it ev - 'ry time. You'll hear the danc - ers' feet, an eas - y shuf - fle. Boy, it

real - ly is a treat, no nois - y scuf - fle sor - ta rid - in' with the beat._____

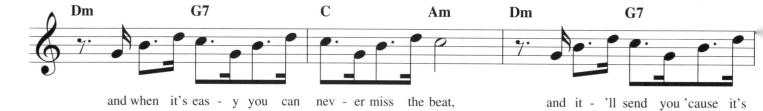

___ Eas - y does ___ it. Watch 'em fall in line. ___ Rhy - thm's for the feet,

and when it's eas - y you can nev - er miss the beat, and it - 'll send you 'cause it's

sol - id - ly a treat._____ Eas - y does ___ it all the time.

FIVE MINUTES MORE

Lyric by SAMMY CAHN
Music by JULE STYNE

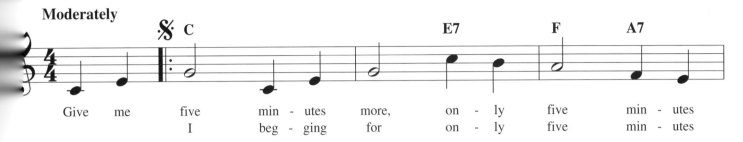

Give me five min-utes more, on-ly five min-utes
I beg-ging for on-ly five min-utes

more, let me stay, ___ let me stay ___ in your arms. ___
more, on-ly five ___ min-utes more __

___ Here am ___ of your charms. ___

All week long I dreamed a-bout our Sat-ur-day date. ___

Don't you know that Sun-day morn-ing you can sleep late? ___ Give me

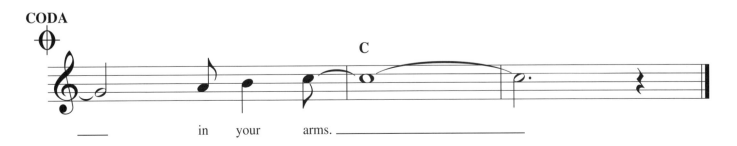

___ in your arms. ___

EASY STREET

By ALAN RANKIN JO

Eas - y Street, _ I'd love to live on Eas - y Street, _

no - bod - y works on Eas - y Street, _ just sit a - round all

day, just sit and play the hors - es. Life is sweet _

for folks who live on Eas - y Street, _ no week - ly pay - ments

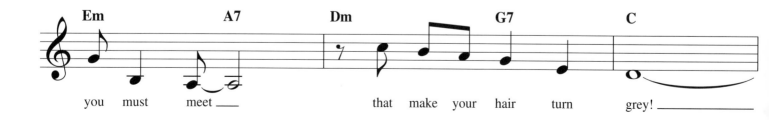

you must meet ___ that make your hair turn grey! ___

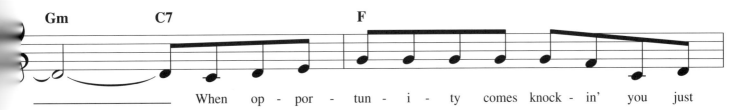

When op - por - tun - i - ty comes knock - in' you just

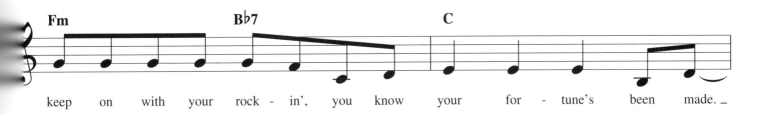

keep on with your rock - in', you know your for - tune's been made. _

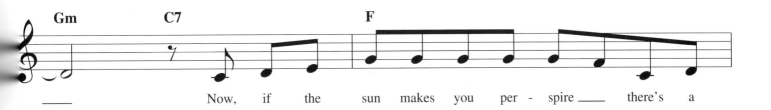

___ Now, if the sun makes you per - spire ___ there's a

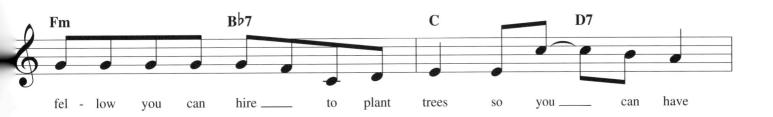

fel - low you can hire ___ to plant trees so you ___ can have

shade on Eas - y Street. _ I'm tell - ing ev - 'ry

one I meet ___ if I could live on Eas - y Street _ I

would - n't want no job to - day, so please go 'way.

EV'RY TIME WE SAY GOODBYE
from SEVEN LIVELY ARTS

Words and Mus
COLE POR

Slowly

Ev - 'ry time ____ we say good - bye I die ____ a lit - tle.

Ev - 'ry time ____ we say good - bye ____ I won - der

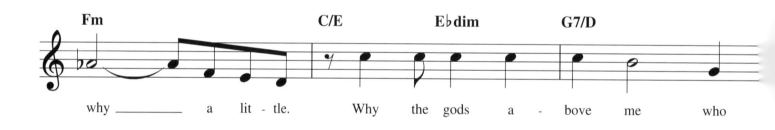

why ____ a lit - tle. Why the gods a - bove me who

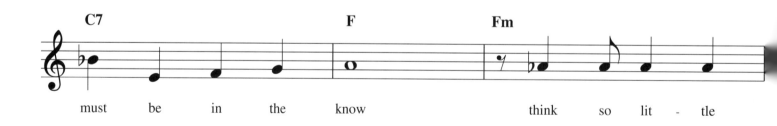

must be in the know think so lit - tle

of me they al - low you to go. ____

49

When you're near _____ there's such an air of spring _____ a - bout it.

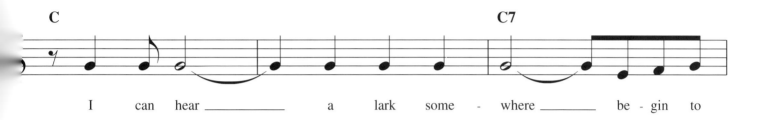

I can hear _____ a lark some - where _____ be - gin to

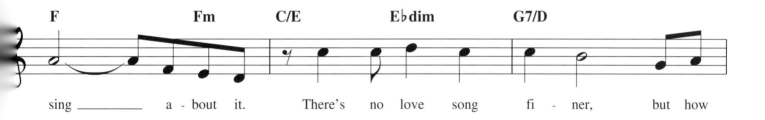

sing _____ a - bout it. There's no love song fi - ner, but how

strange the change from ma - jor to mi - nor ev - 'ry time _____

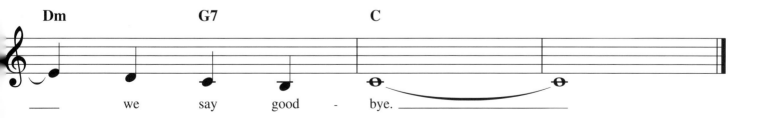

_____ we say good - bye. _____

(I Love You)
FOR SENTIMENTAL REASONS
from AS GOOD AS IT GETS

Words by DEEK WAT
Music by WILLIAM E

Moderately

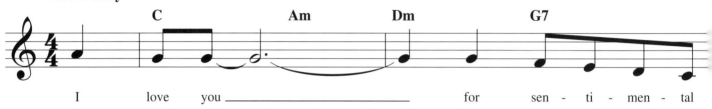

I love you _____ for sen - ti - men - tal

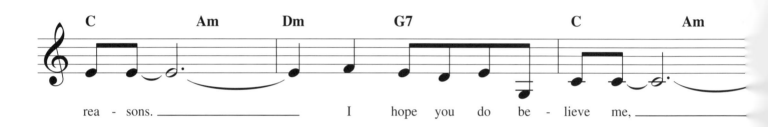

rea - sons. _____ I hope you do be - lieve me, _____

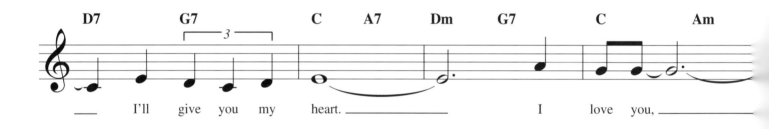

_____ I'll give you my heart. _____ I love you, _____

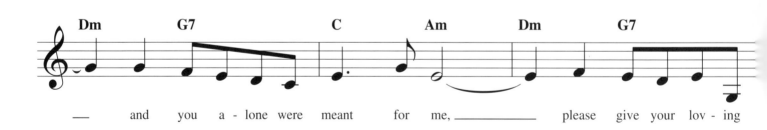

_____ and you a - lone were meant for me, _____ please give your lov - ing

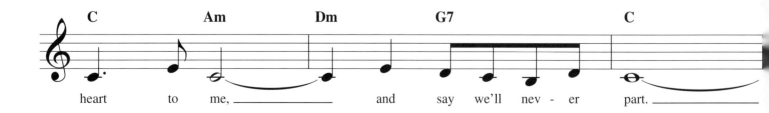

heart to me, _____ and say we'll nev - er part. _____

51

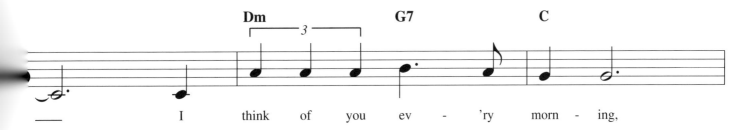

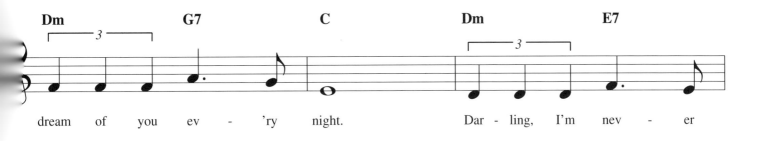

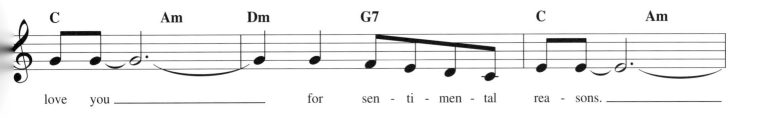

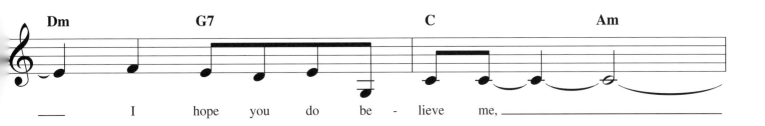

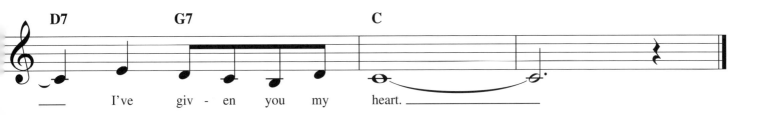

FOR YOU, FOR ME, FOR EVERMORE

Music and Lyrics by GEORGE GERS
and IRA GERS

Slowly

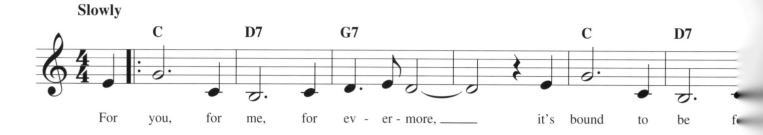

For you, for me, for ev - er - more, _____ it's bound to be f...

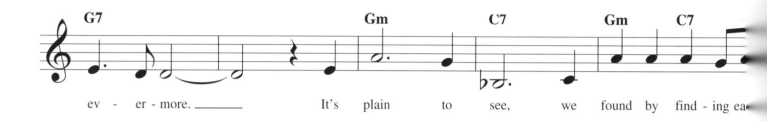

ev - er - more. _____ It's plain to see, we found by find - ing ea...

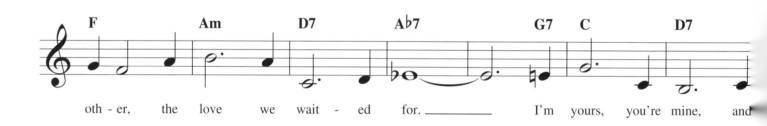

oth - er, the love we wait - ed for. _____ I'm yours, you're mine, and

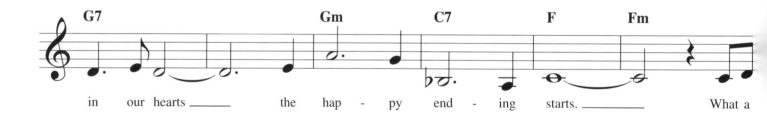

in our hearts _____ the hap - py end - ing starts. _____ What a

love - ly world this world will be, with a world of love in store for

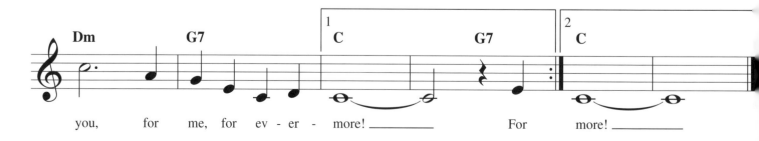

you, for me, for ev - er - more! _____ For more! _____

THE GIRL THAT I MARRY
from the Stage Production ANNIE GET YOUR GUN

Words and Music by
IRVING BERLIN

The girl that I mar - ry will have to be as soft and as pink as a nurs - er - y. The girl I call my own _____ will wear sat - ins and lac - es and smell of col - ogne. Her nails will be pol - ished and in her hair, she'll wear a gar - den - ia and I'll be there. 'Stead of flit - tin' _____ I'll be sit - tin' _____ next to her and she'll purr like a kit - ten. _____ A doll I can car - ry, the girl that I mar - ry must be. _____

1.

2. The be. _____

FRENESÍ

Words and Mus
ALBERTO DOMINC

Medium Latin

It was Fi - es - ta down in Mex - i - co, _____ And so I stopped a - while to
Quie - ro que vi - vas só - lo pa - ra mí _____ y que tú va - yas por don

see the show, _____ I knew that Fre - ne - sí meant "please love me"
de yo voy, _____ pa - ra que mi al - ma sea no más de ti,

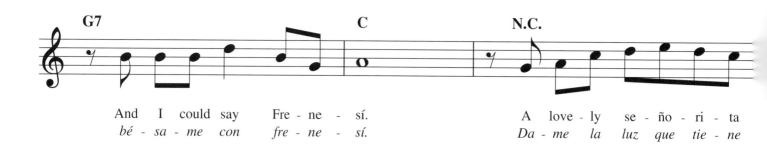

And I could say Fre - ne - sí. A love - ly se - ño - ri - ta
bé - sa - me con fre - ne - sí. Da - me la luz que tie - ne

caught my eye, _____ I stood en - chant - ed as she wan - der'd by, _____
tu mi - rar _____ y la an - sie - dad que en - tre tus la - bios vi,

_____ And nev - er know - ing that it came from me I gen - tly sighed Fre - ne - sí.
_____ e - sa lo - cu - ra de vi - vir y a - mar, que es más que a - mor, fre - ne - sí.

She stopped and raised her eyes to mine,
Hay en el be - so que te dí,

Her lips just plead - ed to be
al - ma, pie - dad, co - ra -

kissed,
zón;

Her eyes were soft as can - dle - shine,
di - me que sa - bes tu sen - tir,

So how was I to re - sist? _____ And now with - out a heart to
lo mis - mo que sien - to yo. _____ Quie - ro que vi - vas só - lo

call my own, _____ A great - er hap - pi - ness I've nev - er known _____
pa - ra mí _____ y que tú va - yas por don - de yo voy, _____

_____ Be - cause her kiss - es are for me a - lone,
_____ pa - ra que mi al - ma sea no más de tí,

Who would-n't say Fre - ne -
bé - sa - me con fre - ne -

sí, _____ who would-n't say Fre - nc - sí! _____
sí, _____ bé - sa - me con fre - ne - sí. _____

HARLEM NOCTURNE

Music by EARLE HA...
Words by DICK RO...

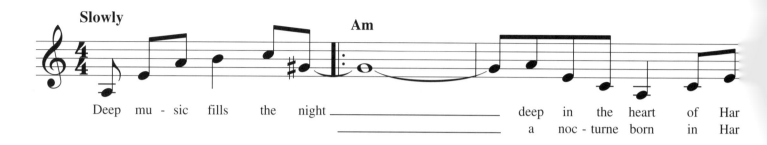

Deep mu - sic fills the night ____ deep in the heart of Har
____ a noc - turne born in Har

- lem ____ and tho' the stars are bright ____
- lem ____ that mel - an - chol - y strain ____

____ the dark - ness is taunt - ing me. ____ Oh! what a sad re - frain __
____ for - ev - er is haunt - ing me. __

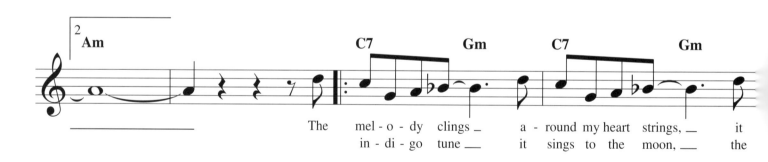

____ The mel - o - dy clings _ a - round my heart strings, _ it
in - di - go tune _ it sings to the moon, _ the

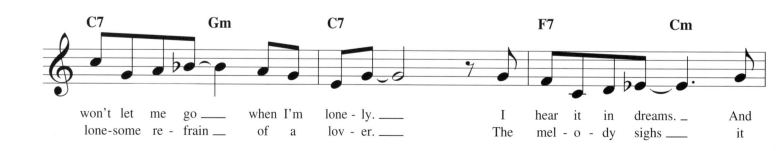

won't let me go ____ when I'm lone - ly. ____ I hear it in dreams. _ And
lone-some re - frain _ of a lov - er. ____ The mel - o - dy sighs ____ it

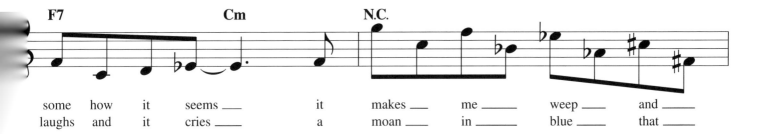

some how it seems ___ it makes ___ me ___ weep ___ and ___
laughs and it cries ___ a moan ___ in ___ blue ___ that ___

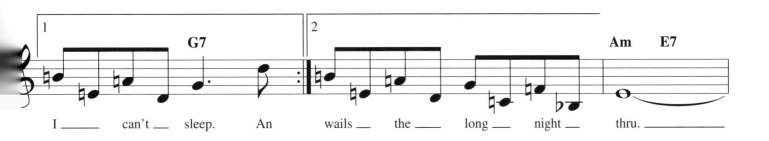

I ___ can't ___ sleep. An wails ___ the ___ long ___ night ___ thru. _____

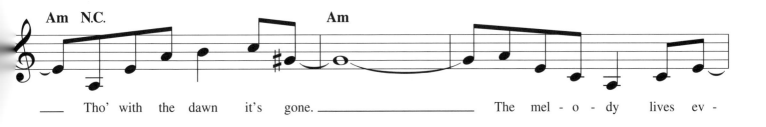

___ Tho' with the dawn it's gone. _____ The mel - o - dy lives ev -

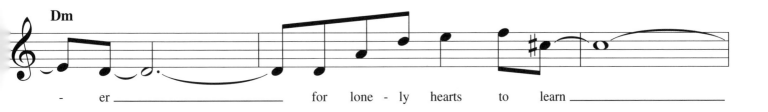

- er _____ for lone - ly hearts to learn _____

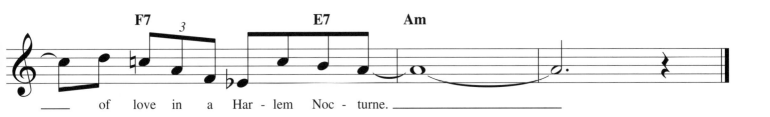

___ of love in a Har - lem Noc - turne. _____

HAVE I TOLD YOU LATELY THAT I LOVE YOU

Words and Music
SCOTT WISE

Have I told you late - ly that I
told you late - ly how I
told you late - ly when I'm

love you? _____ Could I tell you
miss you _____ when the stars are
sleep - ing _____ ev - 'ry dream I

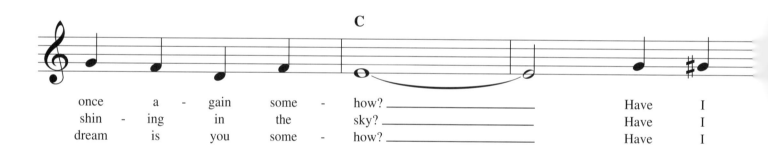

once a - gain some - how? _____ Have I
shin - ing in the sky? _____ Have I
dream is you some - how? _____ Have I

told with all my heart and soul how I a -
told you why the nights are long when you're not
told you who I'd like to share my love for -

dore you? Well, dar - ling, I'm tell - ing you
with me? Well, dar - ling, I'm tell - ing you
ev - er? Well, dar - ling, I'm tell - ing you

now. _____
now. _____
now. _____ } This heart would break in two if you re -

fuse me. _____ I'm no good with - out you an - y -

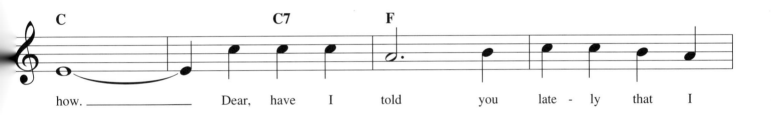

how. _____ Dear, have I told you late - ly that I

love you? _____ Well, dar - ling, I'm tell - ing you

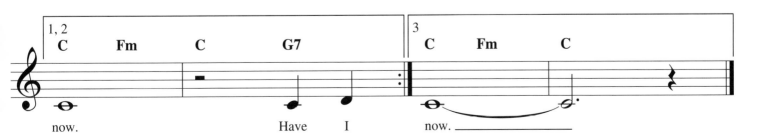

now. Have I now. _____

HOW ARE THINGS IN GLOCCA MORRA

from FINIAN'S RAINBOW

Words by E.Y. HARBU
Music by BURTON LA

Slowly

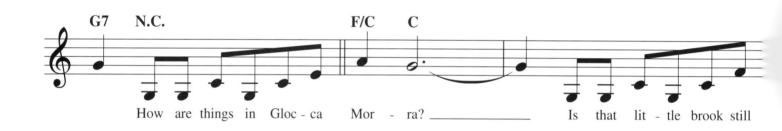

How are things in Gloc - ca Mor - ra? _____ Is that lit - tle brook still

leap - ing there? _____ Does it still run down to Don - ny - cove _____ Through

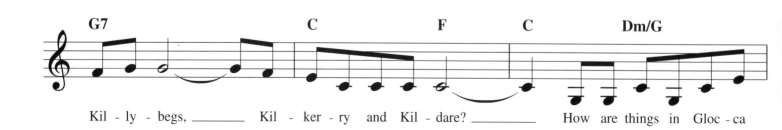

Kil - ly - begs, _____ Kil - ker - ry and Kil - dare? _____ How are things in Gloc - ca

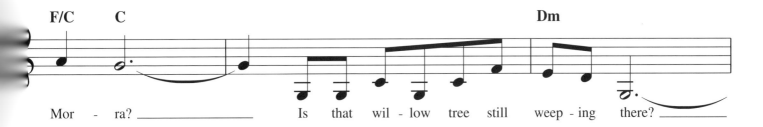

Mor - ra? _____ Is that wil - low tree still weep - ing there? _____

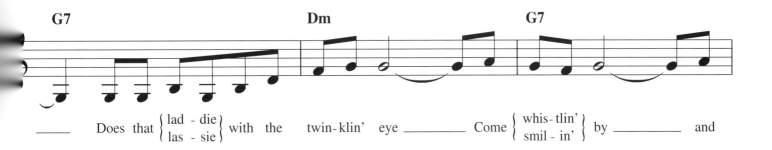

_____ Does that {lad - die / las - sie} with the twin-klin' eye _____ Come {whis - tlin' / smil - in'} by _____ and

does {he / she} walk a - way, Sad and dream-y there not to see me there? _____ So I

ask each weep - in' wil - low and each brook a - long the way, And each

{lad / lass} that comes {a - whis - tlin' / a - sigh - in'} Too - ra - lay, _____ "How are

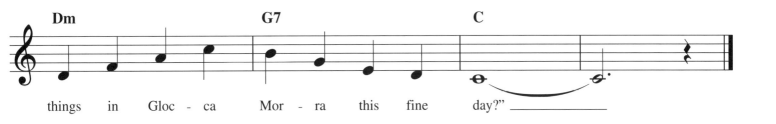

things in Gloc - ca Mor - ra this fine day?" _____

HOW HIGH THE MOON
from TWO FOR THE SHOW

Words by NANCY HAMIL
Music by MORGAN LE

Medium Swing

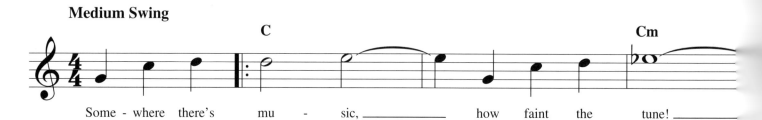

Some - where there's mu - sic, _____ how faint the tune! _____

_____ Some - where there's heav - en, _____ how high the

moon! _____ There is no moon a - bove when

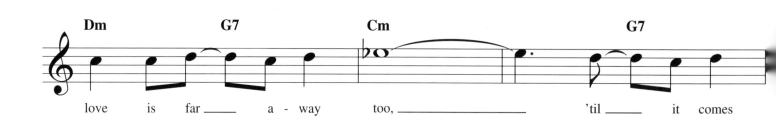

love is far ____ a - way too, _____ 'til ____ it comes

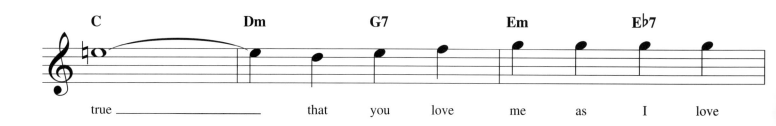

true _____ that you love me as I love

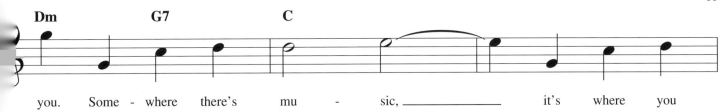

you. Some - where there's mu - sic, _____ it's where you

are. _____ Some - where there's heav - en, _____

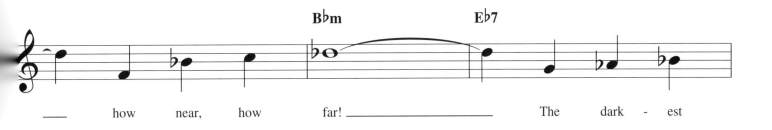

____ how near, how far! _____ The dark - est

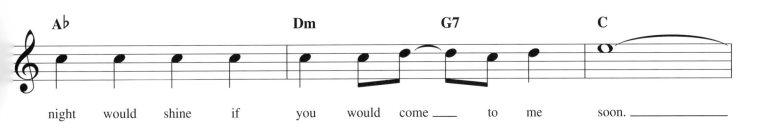

night would shine if you would come ____ to me soon. _____

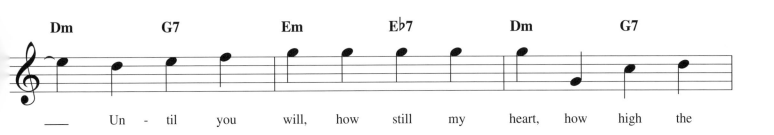

____ Un - til you will, how still my heart, how high the

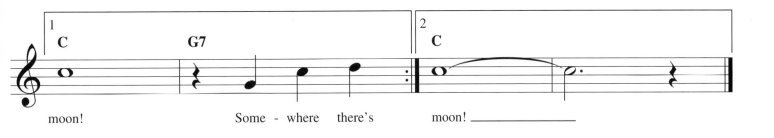

moon! Some - where there's   moon! _____

THE HUCKLEBUCK

Lyrics by ROY ALF
Music by ANDY GIB

Medium Swing

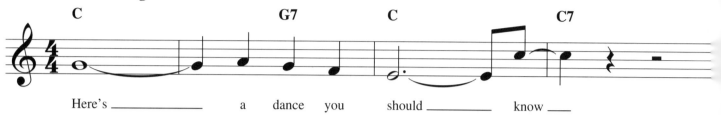

Here's _____ a dance you should _____ know ___

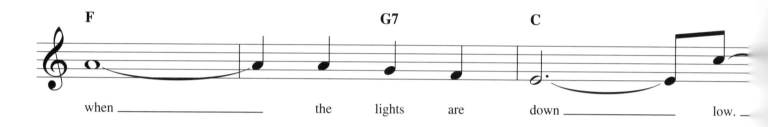

when _____ the lights are down _____ low. _

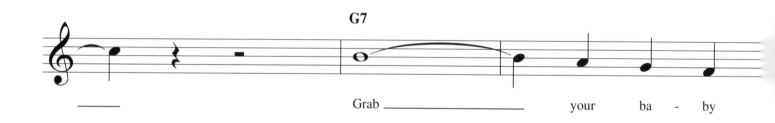

___ Grab _____ your ba - by

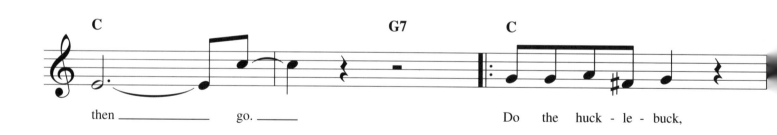

then _____ go. _____ Do the huck - le - buck,

do the huck - le - buck, if you don't know how to do it,

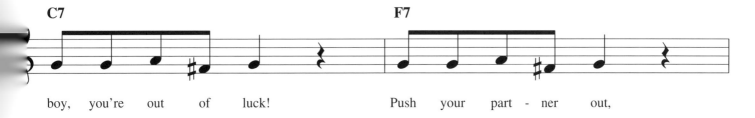

boy, you're out of luck! Push your part - ner out,

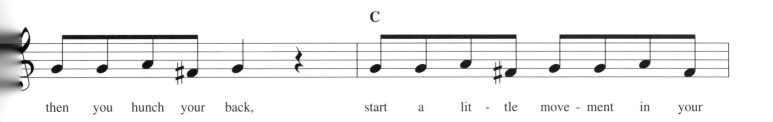

then you hunch your back, start a lit - tle move - ment in your

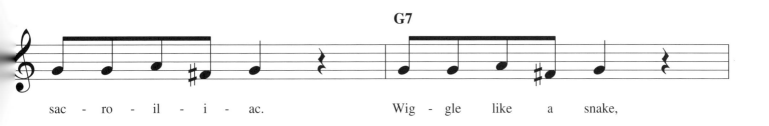

sac - ro - il - i - ac. Wig - gle like a snake,

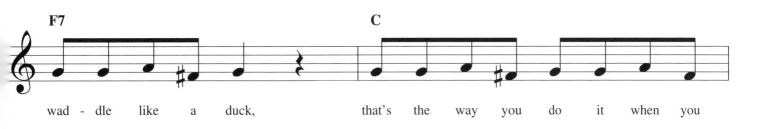

wad - dle like a duck, that's the way you do it when you

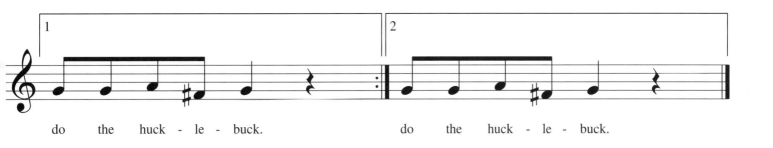

do the huck - le - buck. do the huck - le - buck.

I DON'T WANT TO WALK WITHOUT YOU
from the Paramount Picture SWEATER GIRL

Words by FRANK LOES
Music by JULE ST

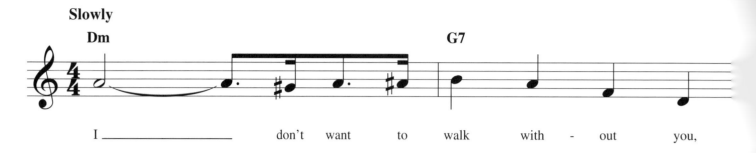

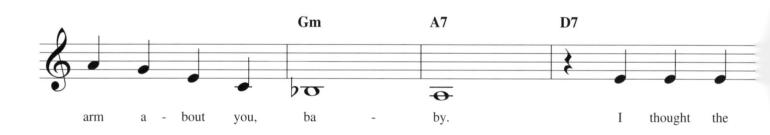

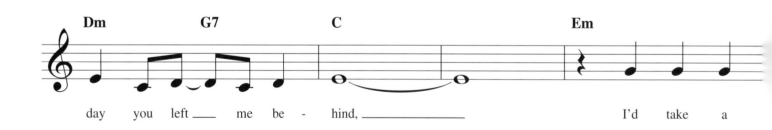

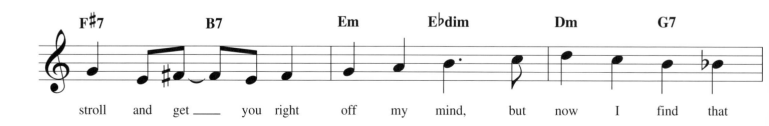

I _____ don't want to walk with - out the sun -

shine. Why'd _____ you have to turn off all that

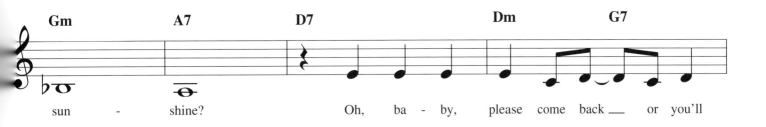

sun - shine? Oh, ba - by, please come back __ or you'll

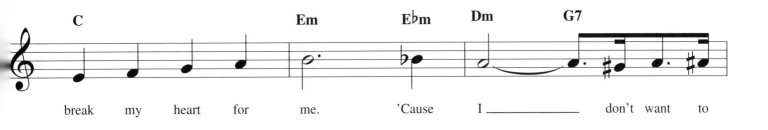

break my heart for me. 'Cause I _____ don't want to

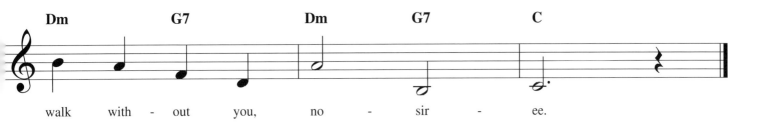

walk with - out you, no - sir - ee.

I GOT IT BAD AND THAT AIN'T GOOD

Words by PAUL FRANCIS WEB...
Music by DUKE ELLING...

Moderately

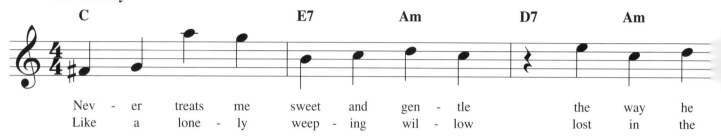

Nev - er treats me sweet and gen - tle the way he
Like a lone - ly weep - ing wil - low lost in the

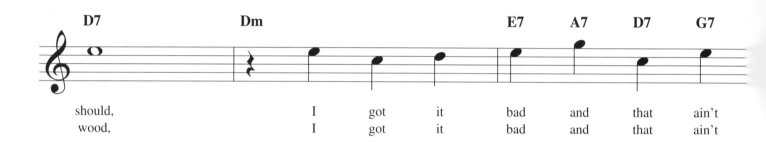

should, I got it bad and that ain't
wood, I got it bad and that ain't

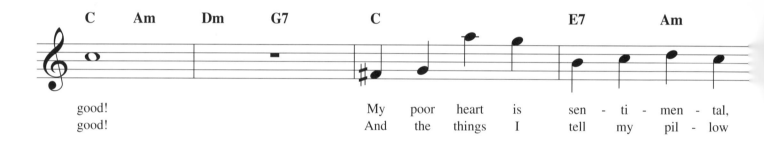

good! My poor heart is sen - ti - men - tal,
good! And the things I tell my pil - low

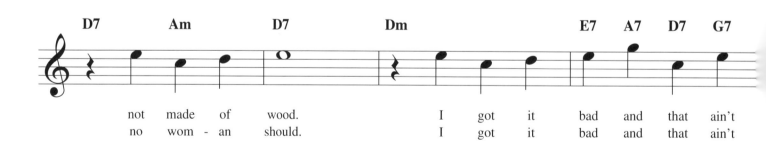

not made of wood. I got it bad and that ain't
no wom - an should. I got it bad and that ain't

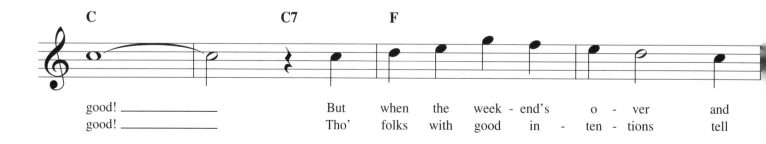

good! _____ But when the week - end's o - ver and
good! _____ Tho' folks with good in - ten - tions tell

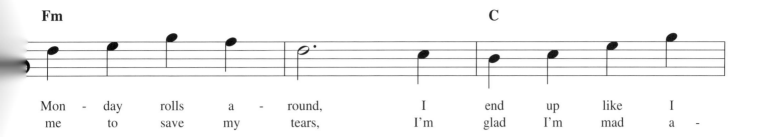

Fm ... C

Mon - day rolls a - round, I end up like I
me to save my tears, I'm glad I'm mad a -

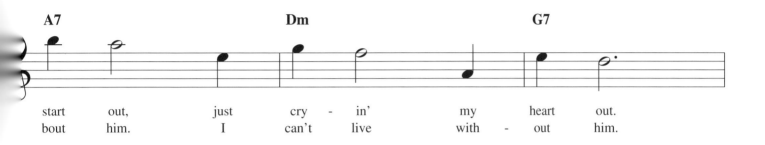

A7 ... Dm ... G7

start out, just cry - in' my heart out.
bout him. I can't live with - out him.

C ... E7 ... Am ... D7 ... Am

He don't love me like I love him, no - bod - y
Lord a - bove me, make him love me the way he

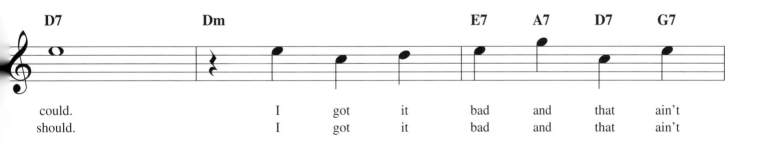

D7 ... Dm ... E7 ... A7 ... D7 ... G7

could. I got it bad and that ain't
should. I got it bad and that ain't

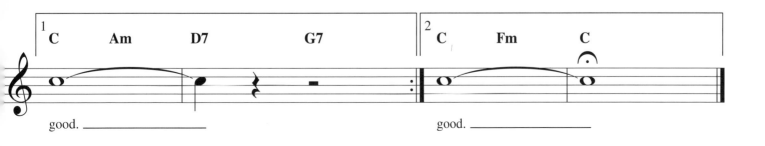

1. C ... Am ... D7 ... G7   2. C ... Fm ... C

good. _____   good. _____

I GOT THE SUN IN THE MORNING
from the Stage Production ANNIE GET YOUR GUN

Words and Mu
IRVING BE

Medium jump tempo

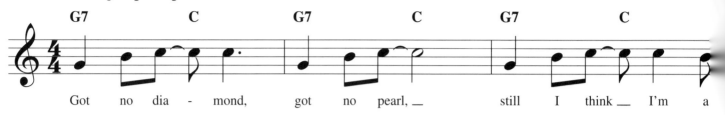

Got no dia - mond, got no pearl, ___ still I think ___ I'm a

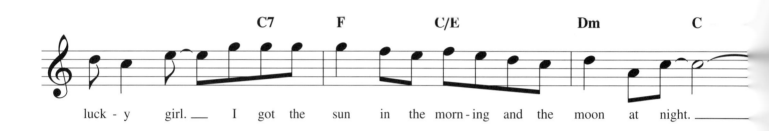

luck - y girl. ___ I got the sun in the morn-ing and the moon at night. ___

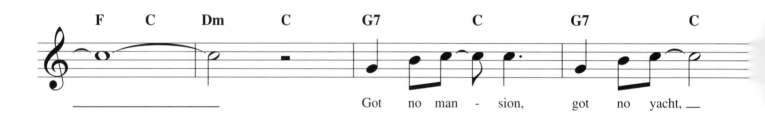

___ Got no man - sion, got no yacht, ___

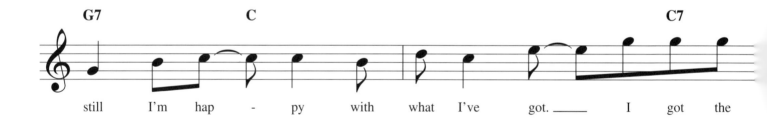

still I'm hap - py with what I've got. ___ I got the

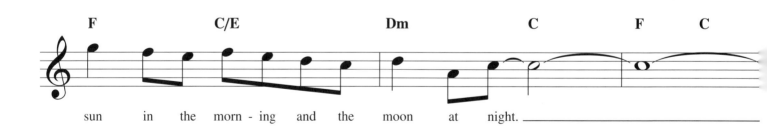

sun in the morn - ing and the moon at night. ___

___ Sun - shine ___ gives me a love -

A7   **D7**

- ly day. _____   Moon - light _____

G7

____ gives me the milk - y way. _____

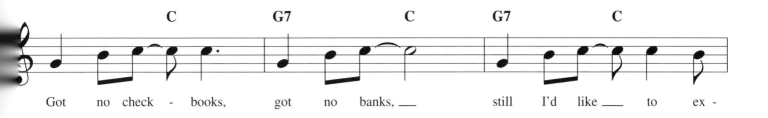

C   **G7**   **C**   **G7**   **C**

Got no check - books, got no banks, ___ still I'd like ___ to ex -

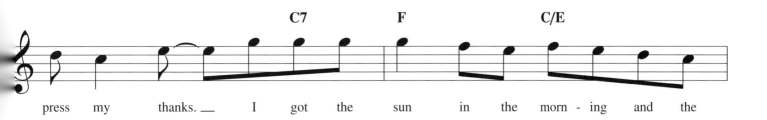

C7   **F**   **C/E**

press my thanks. __ I got the sun in the morn - ing and the

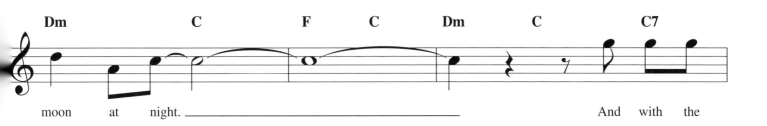

Dm   **C**   **F**   **C**   **Dm**   **C**   **C7**

moon at night. _____ And with the

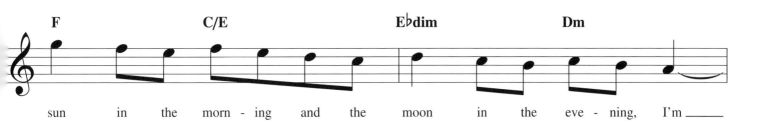

F   **C/E**   **E♭dim**   **Dm**

sun in the morn - ing and the moon in the eve - ning, I'm ____

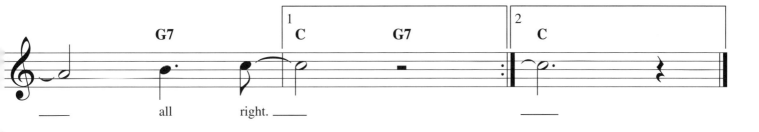

G7 |1 **C**   **G7** |2 **C**

___ all right. ___

I HEAR MUSIC
from the Paramount Picture DANCING ON A DIME

Words by FRANK LOES
Music by BURTON L

I STILL GET JEALOUS
from the Broadway Musical HIGH BUTTON SHOES

MORLEY MUSIC CO.
ght Renewed, Assigned to MORLEY MUSIC CO. and CAHN MUSIC COMPANY
for CAHN MUSIC COMPANY Administered by CHERRY LANE MUSIC PUBLISHING COMPANY, INC.
DREAMWORKS SONGS
hts outside the United States Controlled by MORLEY MUSIC CO.
hts Reserved

Lyric by SAMMY CAHN
Music by JULE STYNE

Slowly

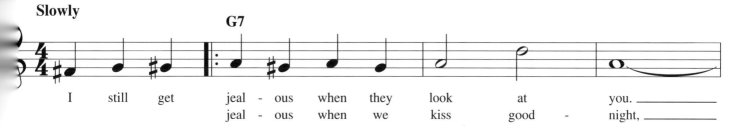

I still get jeal - ous when they look at you. ____
jeal - ous when we kiss good - night, ____

____ I may not show it, but I do. ____
____ un - less you hold me ex - tra tight. ____

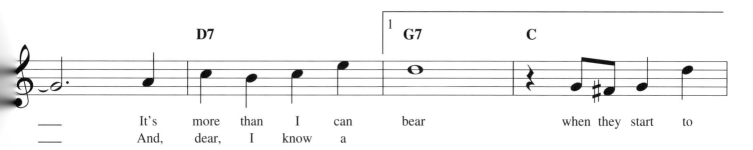

____ It's more than I can bear when they start to
____ And, dear, I know a

stare. Guess they think you're too good to be true. ____

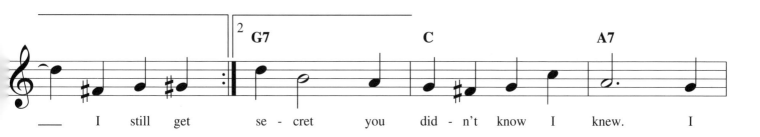

____ I still get se - cret you did - n't know I knew. I

still get jeal - ous 'cause it pleas - es you. ____

I REMEMBER YOU

from the Paramount Picture THE FLEET'S IN

Words by JOHNNY MER—
Music by VICTOR SCHERTZIN—

Moderately

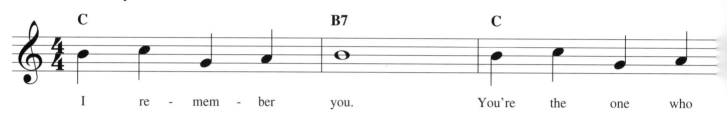

I re - mem - ber you. You're the one who

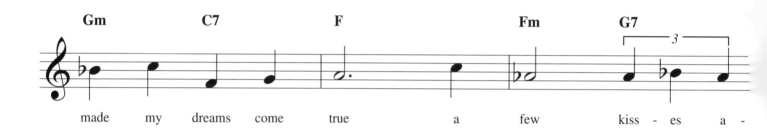

made my dreams come true a few kiss - es a -

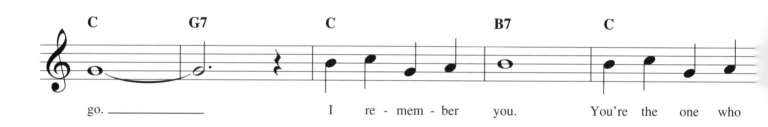

go. ___ I re - mem - ber you. You're the one who

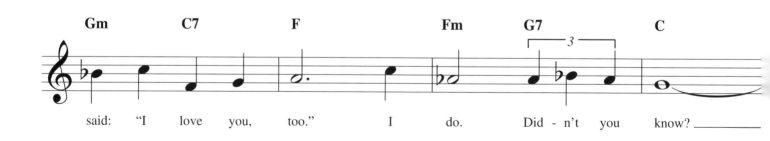

said: "I love you, too." I do. Did - n't you know? ___

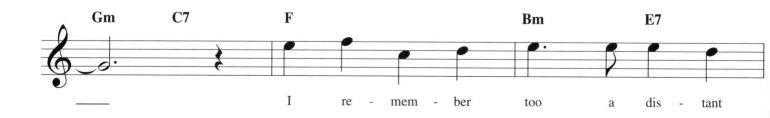

___ I re - mem - ber too a dis - tant

bell   and stars that fell   like rain,   out of the

blue. _____ When my life is through

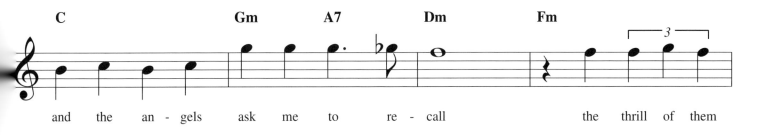

and the an - gels ask me to re - call   the thrill of them

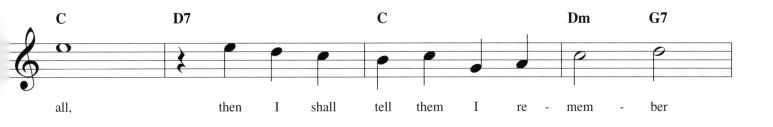

all,   then I shall tell them I re - mem - ber

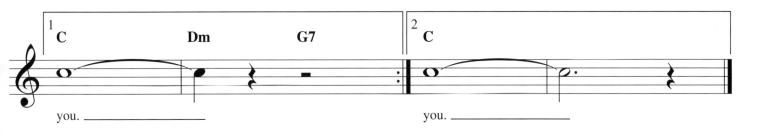

you. _____   you. _____

I SAID MY PAJAMAS (AND PUT ON MY PRAY'RS)

Words and Music by EDDIE P
and GEORGE W

Rhythmically

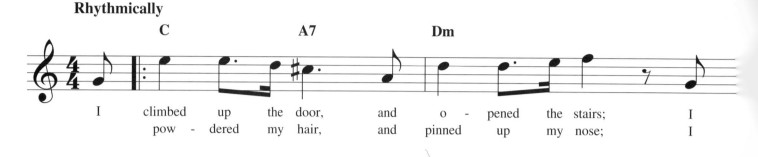

I climbed up the door, and o-pened the stairs; I
pow-dered my hair, and pinned up my nose; I

said my pa-ja-mas, and put on my pray'rs. I
hung up the bath, and I turned on my clothes. I

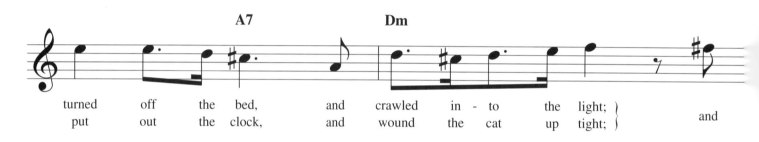

turned off the bed, and crawled in-to the light; }
put out the clock, and wound the cat up tight; }
and

all be-cause you kissed me good-night. { Next morn-ing I woke, and
{ I ran up the shade, and

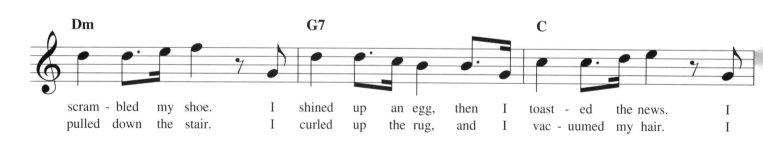

scram-bled my shoe. I shined up an egg, then I toast-ed the news. I
pulled down the stair. I curled up the rug, and I vac-uumed my hair. I

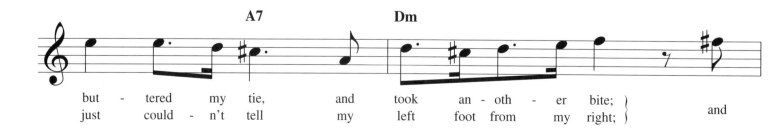

but-tered my tie, and took an-oth-er bite; }
just could-n't tell my left foot from my right; }
and

I WISH I DIDN'T LOVE YOU SO
from the Paramount Picture THE PERILS OF PAULINE

Words and Mus
FRANK LOES

Moderately

I wish I did - n't love you so, _____ my love for

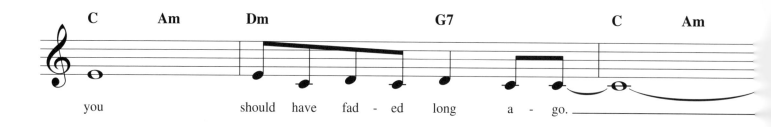

you should have fad - ed long a - go. _____

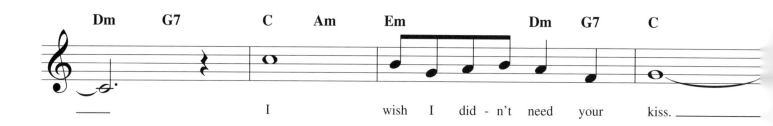

___ I wish I did - n't need your kiss. _____

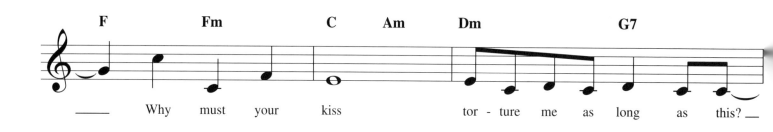

___ Why must your kiss tor - ture me as long as this? _

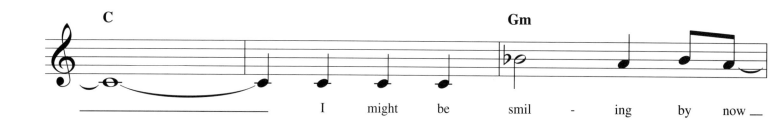

_____ I might be smil - ing by now _

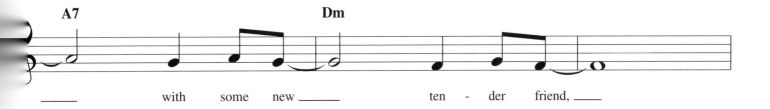

with some new _____ ten - der friend, _____

smil - ing by now _____ with my heart _____ on the mend. __

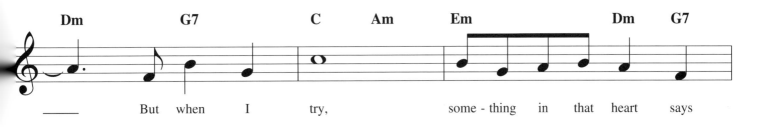

_____ But when I try, some - thing in that heart says

"No," _____ you're still there. I

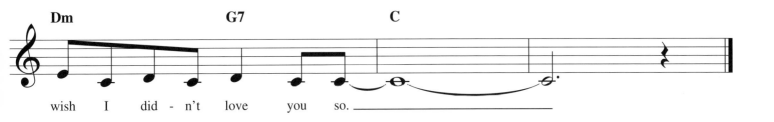

wish I did - n't love you so. _____

I WISH YOU LOVE

English Words by ALBERT BE
French Words and Music by CHARLES TRE

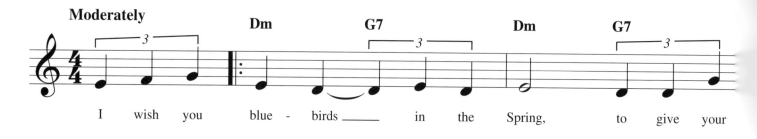

I wish you blue - birds ____ in the Spring, to give your

heart a song to sing; and then a kiss, but more than

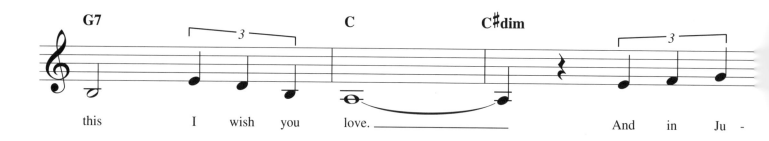

this I wish you love. ____ And in Ju-

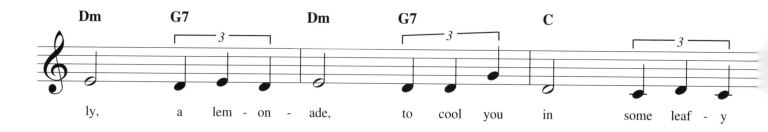

ly, a lem - on - ade, to cool you in some leaf - y

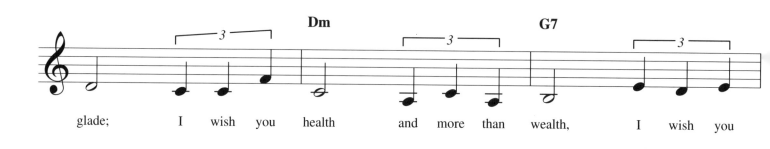

glade; I wish you health and more than wealth, I wish you

love. ____ My break - ing heart and I a-

gree   that you and I   could nev - er be,   so with my

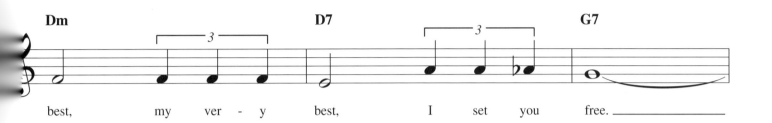

best,   my ver - y best,   I set you free. _____

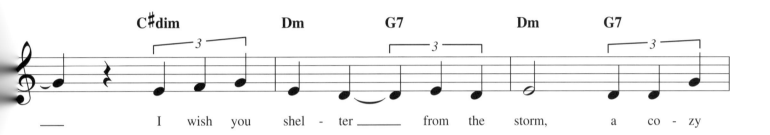

_____ I wish you shel - ter _____ from the storm,   a co - zy

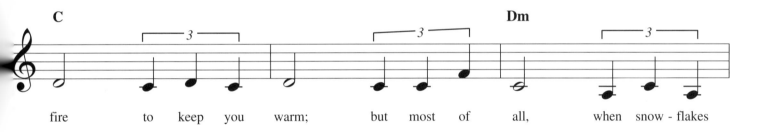

fire   to keep you warm;   but most of all,   when snow - flakes

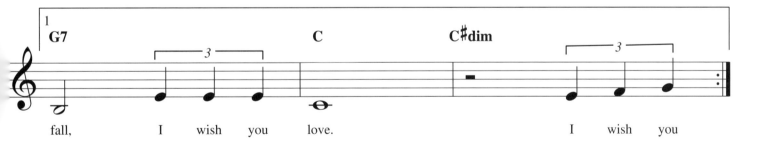

fall,   I wish you love.   I wish you

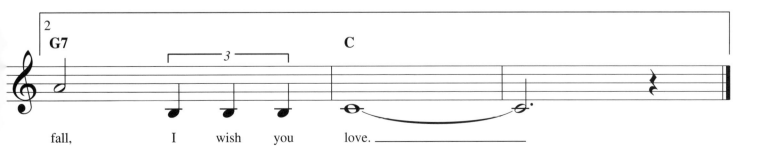

fall,   I wish you love. _____

I'LL NEVER SMILE AGAIN

Words and Music
RUTH LO

I'll nev - er smile a - gain un - til I smile at

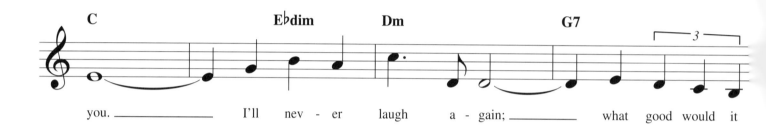

you. _____ I'll nev - er laugh a - gain; _____ what good would it

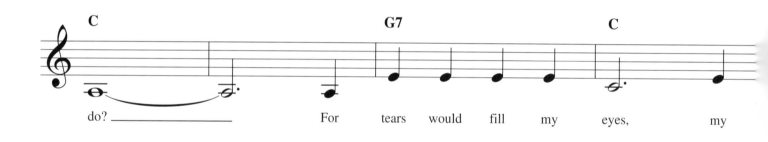

do? _____ For tears would fill my eyes, my

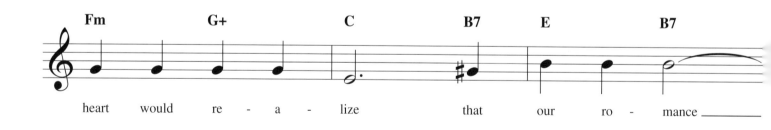

heart would re - a - lize that our ro - mance _____

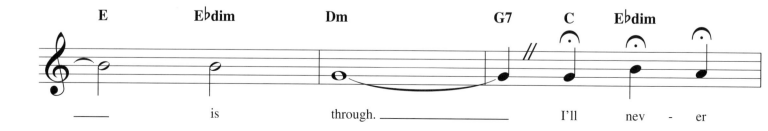

_____ is through. _____ I'll nev - er

love a - gain I'm so in love with you. _____ I'll nev - er

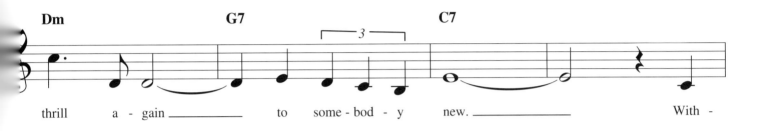

thrill a - gain _____ to some - bod - y new. _____ With -

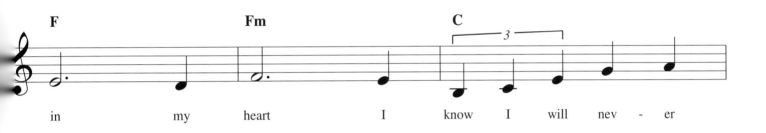

in my heart I know I will nev - er

start to smile a - gain un - til I smile at

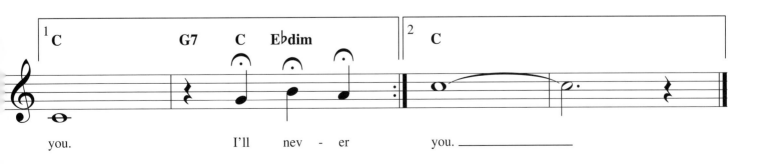

you. I'll nev - er you. _____

I'LL REMEMBER APRIL

Words and Music by PAT JOHN
DON RAYE and GENE DE

Moderately

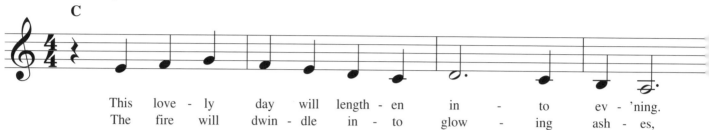

This love - ly day will length - en in - to ev - 'ning.
The fire will dwin - dle in - to glow - ing ash - es,

We'll sigh good - bye to all we've ev - er had. _____
for flames and love live such a lit - tle while. _____

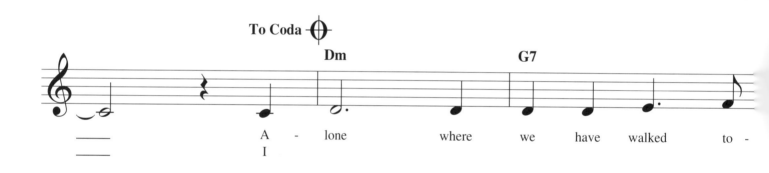

_____ A - lone where we have walked to -
_____ I

geth - er, _____ I'll re - mem - ber A - pril _____

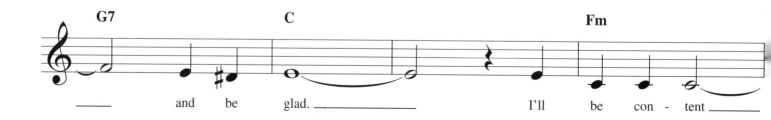

_____ and be glad. _____ I'll be con - tent _____

you loved me once in A - pril. Your lips were warm ____

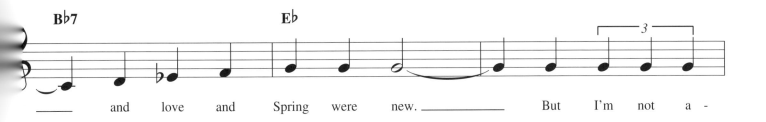

____ and love and Spring were new. ____ But I'm not a -

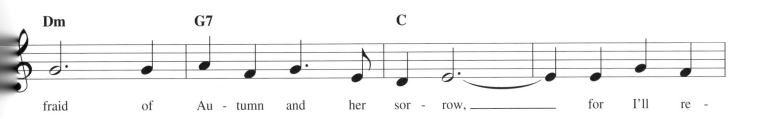

fraid of Au - tumn and her sor - row, ____ for I'll re -

D.C. al Coda

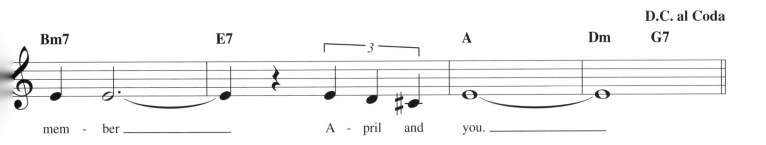

mem - ber ____ A - pril and you. ____

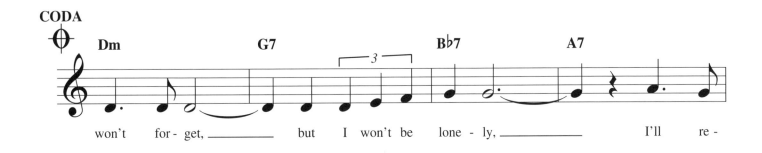

won't for - get, ____ but I won't be lone - ly, ____ I'll re -

mem - ber A - pril, ____ and I'll smile. ____

I'LL WALK ALONE
from the Motion Picture FOLLOW THE BOYS
from WITH A SONG IN MY HEART

Lyric by SAMMY C...
Music by JULE ST...

I'll walk a - lone _____ be - cause, to tell you the truth, __ I'll be
lone, _____ they'll ask me why and I'll tell ___ them I'd

lone - ly. _____ I don't mind be - ing lone - ly ___
rath - er. _____ There are dreams I must gath - er, ___

____ when my heart tells me you _____ are lone - ly
____ dreams we fash - ioned the night _____ you held me

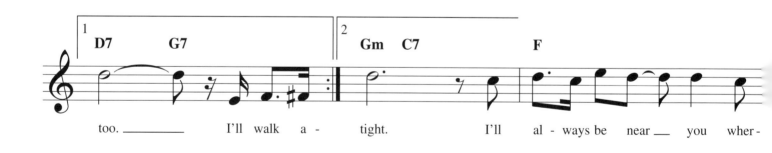

too. _____ I'll walk a -
tight. I'll al - ways be near __ you wher-

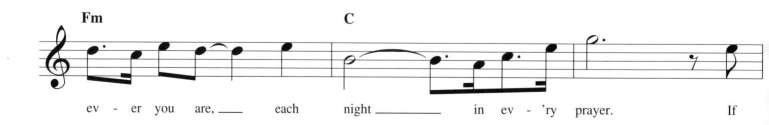

ev - er you are, ___ each night _____ in ev - 'ry prayer. If

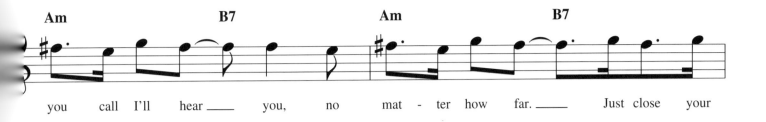

you call I'll hear ___ you, no mat - ter how far. ___ Just close your

eyes _____ and I'll be there. _____ Please walk a -

lone _____ and send your love and your kiss - es to

guide me. _____ Till you're walk - ing be - side ___

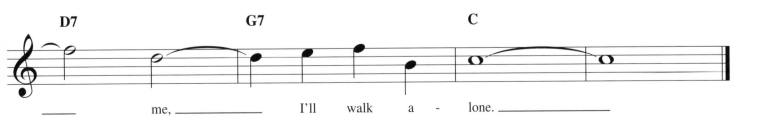

___ me, _____ I'll walk a - lone. _____

I'M BEGINNING TO SEE THE LIGHT

Words and Music by DON GEORGE, JOHNNY HODG
DUKE ELLINGTON and HARRY JA

Medium bounce

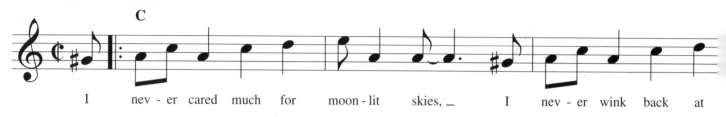

I nev - er cared much for moon - lit skies, __ I nev - er wink back at

fi - re - flies; __ but now that the stars are in your eyes, __ I'm be -

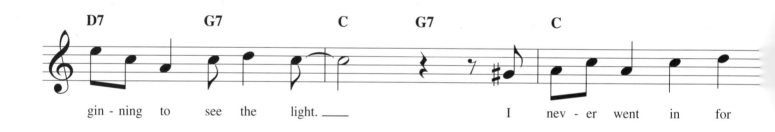

gin - ning to see the light. __ I nev - er went in for

af - ter - glow __ or can - dle - light on the mis - tle - toe, __ but

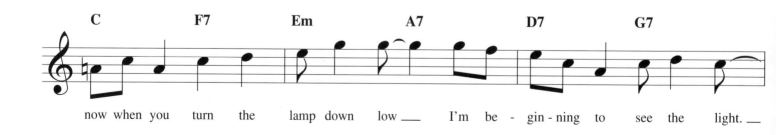

now when you turn the lamp down low __ I'm be - gin - ning to see the light. __

C　　　　　　　　**E7**

_Used to ram - ble thru the park, ___

Eb7　　　　　　　　　　　　**D7**

shad - ow - box - ing in the dark. ___ Then you came and

Ab7　　　　　　　　**G7**

caused a spark ___ that's a four - a - larm fi - re now. ___ I

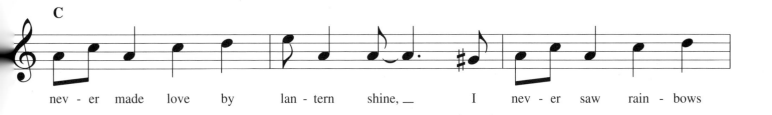

C

nev - er made love by lan - tern shine, ___ I nev - er saw rain - bows

Ab7　　　　　　　　**C**　　**F7**　　**Em**　　**A7**

in my wine; ___ but now that your lips are burn - ing mine, ___ I'm be -

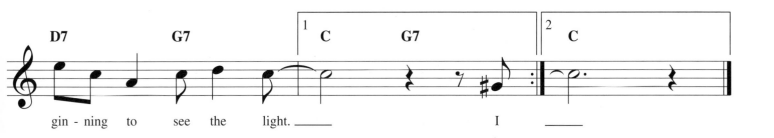

D7　　　　**G7**　　　　**1 C**　　**G7**　　　　**2 C**

gin - ning to see the light. ___ I ___

IF I LOVED YOU
from CAROUSEL

Lyrics by OSCAR HAMMERSTE
Music by RICHARD RODG

Flowing

If I loved you time and a-gain I would try to say

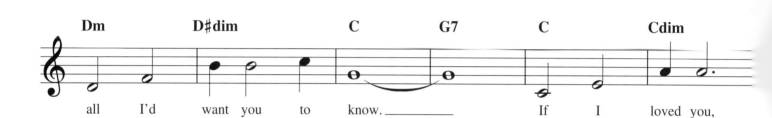

all I'd want you to know. _____ If I loved you,

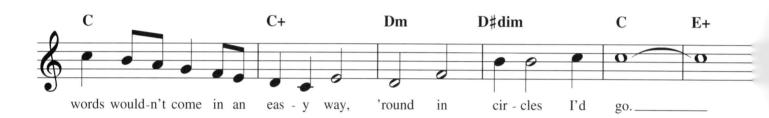

words would-n't come in an eas-y way, 'round in cir-cles I'd go. _____

Long-in' to tell you but a-fraid and shy, I'd let my

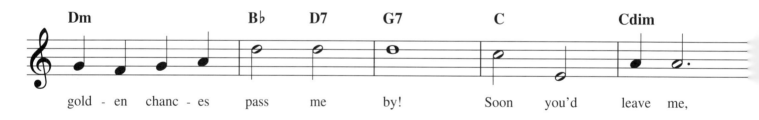

gold-en chanc-es pass me by! Soon you'd leave me,

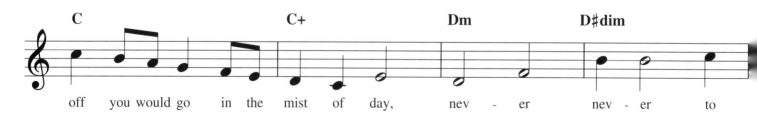

off you would go in the mist of day, nev-er nev-er to

know _____ how I loved you, if I loved you. _____

IT COULD HAPPEN TO YOU
from the Paramount Picture AND THE ANGELS SING

Words by JOHNNY BURKE
Music by JAMES VAN HEUSEN

IS YOU IS, OR IS YOU AIN'T (MA' BABY)
from FOLLOW THE BOYS
from FIVE GUYS NAMED MOE

Words and Music by BILLY AUS
and LOUIS JORD

Is you is, or is you ain't, ma' ba - by?

The way you're act - ing late - ly makes me doubt. ___

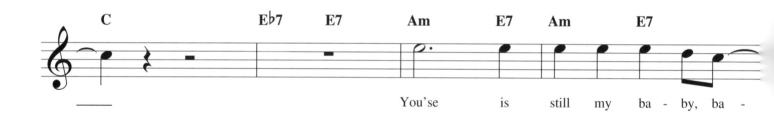

___ You'se is still my ba - by, ba -

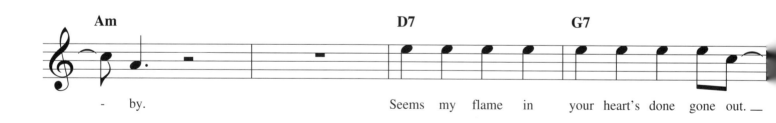

- by.   Seems my flame in your heart's done gone out. ___

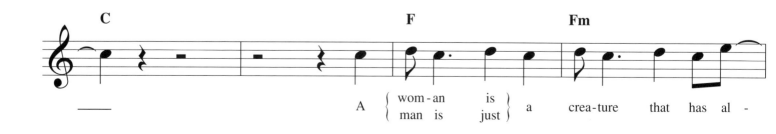

___   A { wom - an is / man is just } a crea - ture that has al -

- ways __ been strange, __ just when you're sure of

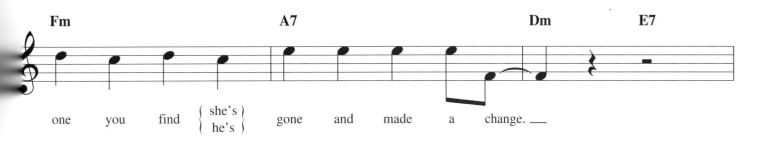

one you find { she's / he's } gone and made a change. __

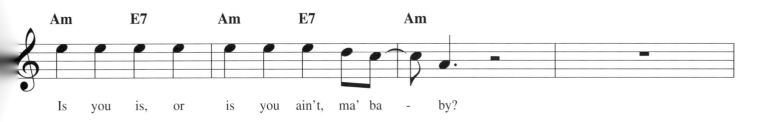

Is you is, or is you ain't, ma' ba - by?

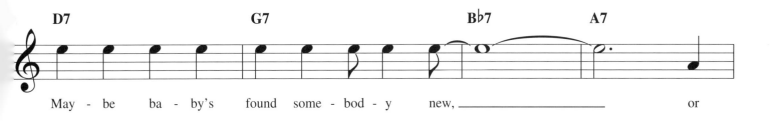

May - be ba - by's found some - bod - y new, _____ or

is ma' ba - by, still ma' ba - by true? __

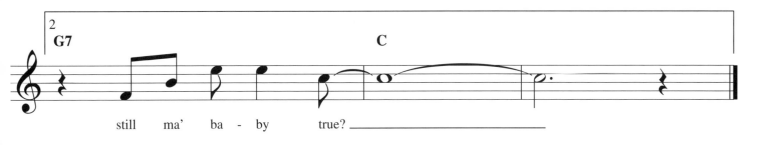

still ma' ba - by true? _____

IT'S A PITY TO SAY GOODNIGHT

Words and Mus
BILLY F

Romantically

It's   a   pit - y   to   say   "good - night" _____ be - cause   I
        pit - y   to   say   "Fare - well" _____ be - cause   the

nev - er saw stars so bright. _____ But if you got - ta go home, __ you got - ta
man in the moon won't tell. _____ But if you got - ta go home, __ you got - ta

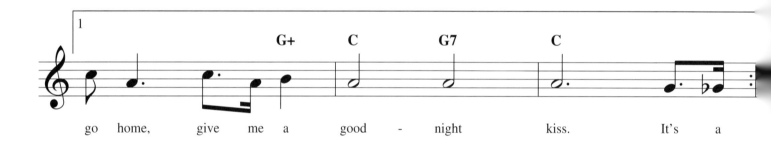

go home, give me a good - night kiss. It's a

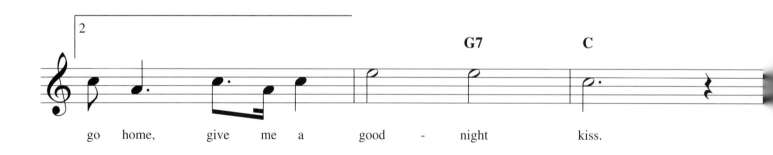

go home, give me a good - night kiss.

How's a - bout to - mor - row night, _____ just

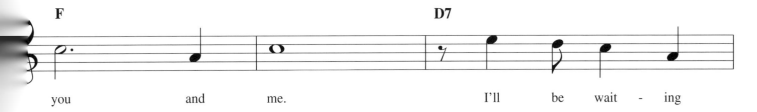

you and me. I'll be wait - ing

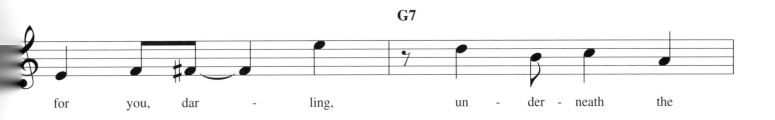

for you, dar - ling, un - der - neath the

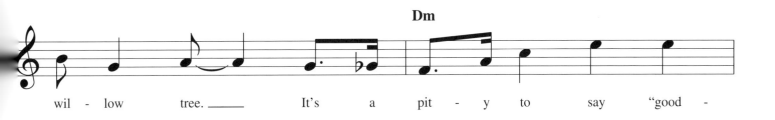

wil - low tree. ____ It's a pit - y to say "good -

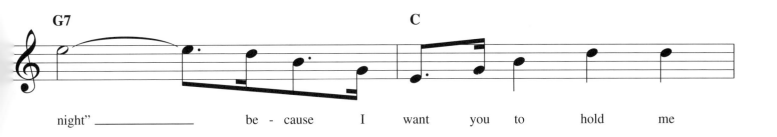

night" _____ be - cause I want you to hold me

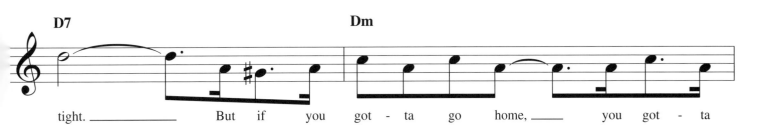

tight. _____ But if you got - ta go home, ____ you got - ta

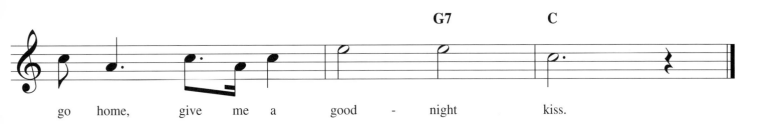

go home, give me a good - night kiss.

IT'S BEEN A LONG, LONG TIME

Lyric by SAMMY C.
Music by JULE ST

Slowly, with a lilt

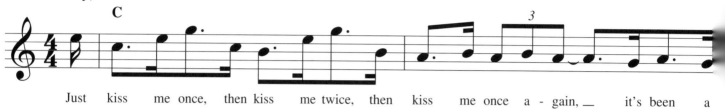

Just kiss me once, then kiss me twice, then kiss me once a - gain, __ it's been a

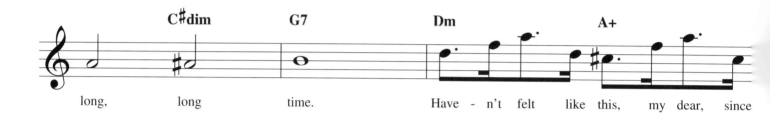

long, long time. Have - n't felt like this, my dear, since

can't re-mem-ber when, __ it's been a long, long time. You'll nev - er

know how man - y dreams I dreamed a - bout you __ or

just how emp - ty they all seemed with - out you. __ So, kiss me once, then kiss me twice, then

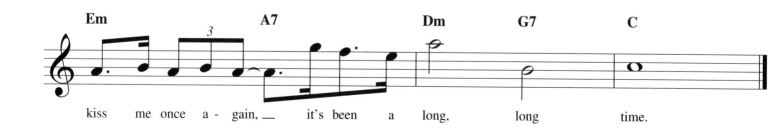

kiss me once a - gain, __ it's been a long, long time.

JINGLE JANGLE JINGLE
(I Got Spurs)
from the Paramount Picture THE FOREST RANGERS

Words by FRANK LOESSER
Music by JOSEPH J. LILLEY

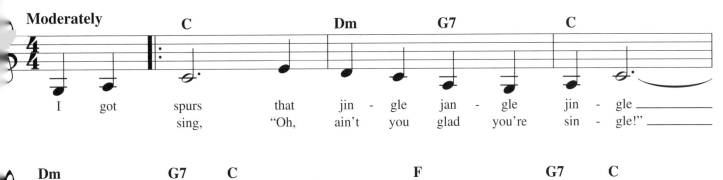

I got spurs that jin - gle jan - gle jin - gle _____
sing, "Oh, ain't you glad you're sin - gle!" _____

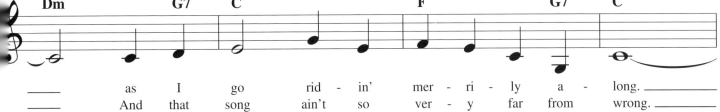

_____ as I go rid - in' mer - ri - ly a - long. _____
_____ And that song ain't so ver - y far from wrong. _____

_____ And they _____ Oh, Lil - lie Belle, _____ oh, Lil - lie

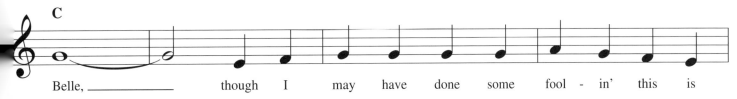

Belle, _____ though I may have done some fool - in' this is

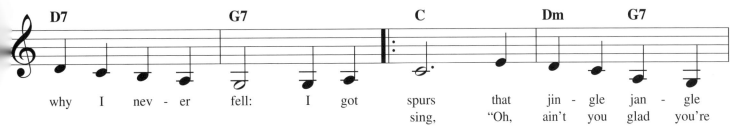

why I nev - er fell: I got spurs that jin - gle jan - gle
sing, "Oh, ain't you glad you're

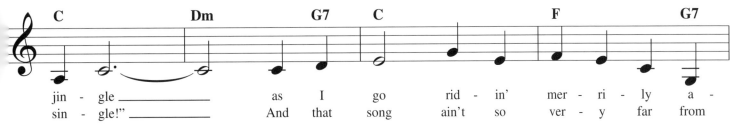

jin - gle _____ as I go rid - in' mer - ri - ly a -
sin - gle!" _____ And that song ain't so ver - y far from

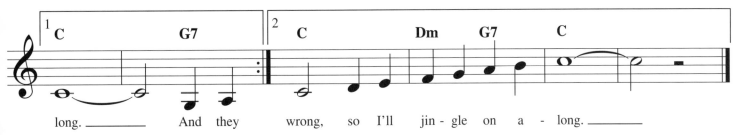

long. _____ And they wrong, so I'll jin - gle on a - long. _____

JAVA JIVE

Words and Music by MILTON DR
and BEN OAKL

Lightly, with an easy beat

1.,3. I love cof-fee, I love tea, ___ I love the ja-va jive and
2.,4. I love ja-va, sweet and hot, ___ whoops! Mis-ter Mo-to, I'm a

it loves me. ___ Cof-fee and tea ___ and the jiv-in' and me, ___ a
cof-fee pot. ___ Shoot me a pot ___ and I'll pour me a shot, ___ a

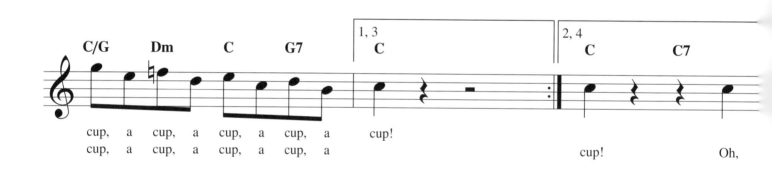

cup, a cup, a cup, a cup, a cup!
cup, a cup, a cup, a cup, a cup! Oh,

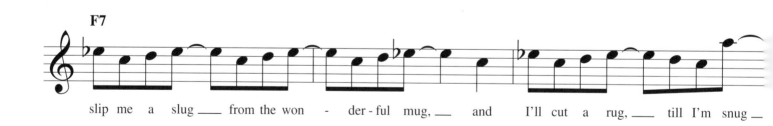

slip me a slug ___ from the won - der-ful mug, ___ and I'll cut a rug, ___ till I'm snug ___

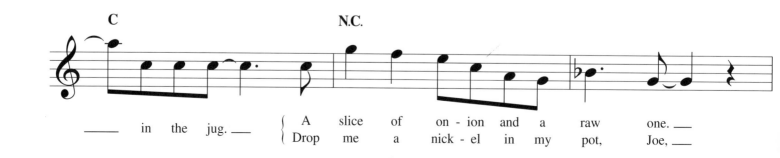

___ in the jug. ___ A slice of on-ion and a raw one. ___
Drop me a nick-el in my pot, Joe, ___

JUNE IS BUSTIN' OUT ALL OVER
from CAROUSEL

Lyrics by OSCAR HAMMERST
Music by RICHARD RODG

Brightly

June   is   bust - in'   out   all   o - ver! _____   All
June   is   bust - in'   out   all   o - ver! _____   The
June   is   bust - in'   out   all   o - ver! _____   The

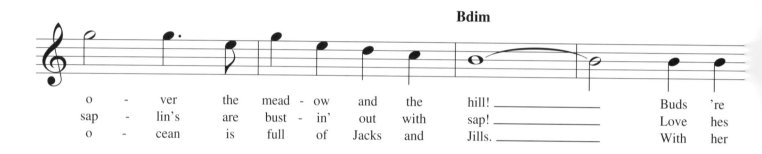

o - ver   the   mead - ow   and   the   hill! _____   Buds   're
sap - lin's   are   bust - in'   out   with   sap! _____   Love   hes
o - cean   is   full   of   Jacks   and   Jills. _____   With   her

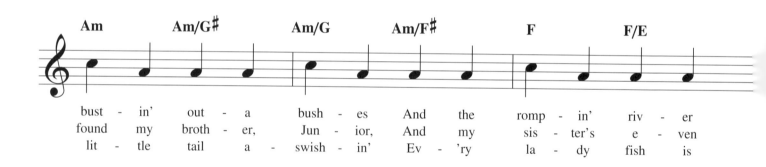

bust - in'   out   a   bush - es   And   the   romp - in'   riv - er
found   my   broth - er,   Jun - ior,   And   my   sis - ter's   e - ven
lit - tle   tail   a - swish - in'   Ev - 'ry   la - dy   fish   is

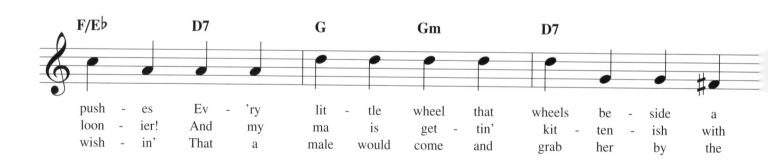

push - es   Ev - 'ry   lit - tle   wheel   that   wheels   be - side   a
loon - ier!   And   my   ma   is   get - tin'   kit - ten - ish   with
wish - in'   That   a   male   would   come   and   grab   her   by   the

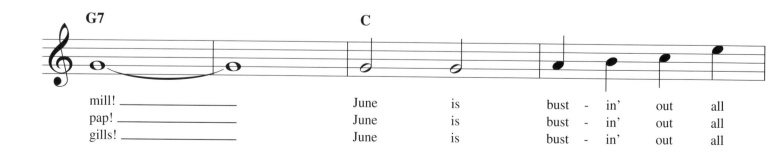

mill! _____   June   is   bust - in'   out   all
pap! _____   June   is   bust - in'   out   all
gills! _____   June   is   bust - in'   out   all

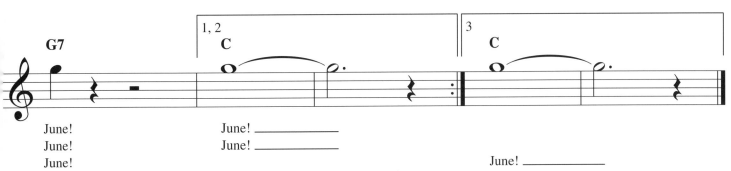

JUST SQUEEZE ME
(But Don't Tease Me)

Words by LEE GA
Music by DUKE ELLING

LET THERE BE LOVE

Lyric by IAN GRANT
Music by LIONEL RAND

THE LAST TIME I SAW PARIS

from LADY, BE GOOD
from TILL THE CLOUDS ROLL BY

Lyrics by OSCAR HAMMERSTE
Music by JEROME K

The last time I saw Par - is her heart was warm and

gay. I heard the laugh - ter of her heart in

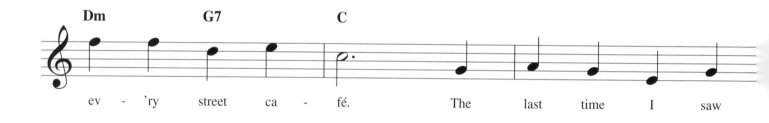

ev - 'ry street ca - fé. The last time I saw

Par - is, her trees were dressed for spring, and

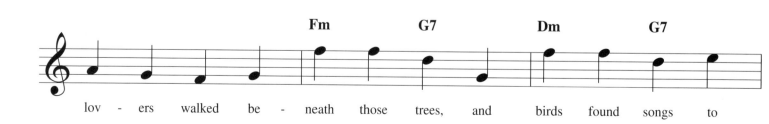

lov - ers walked be - neath those trees, and birds found songs to

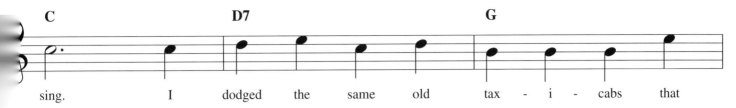

sing.   I   dodged   the   same   old   tax - i - cabs   that

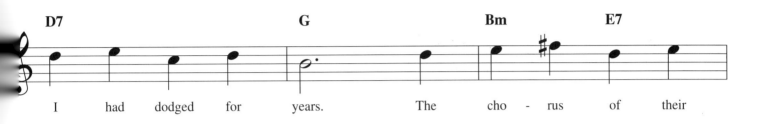

I   had   dodged   for   years.   The   cho - rus   of   their

squeak - y   horns   was   mu - sic   to   my   ears.   The

last   time   I   saw   Par - is,   her   heart   was   warm   and

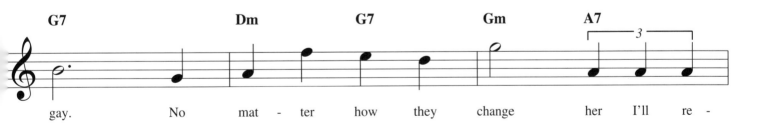

gay.   No   mat - ter   how   they   change   her   I'll   re -

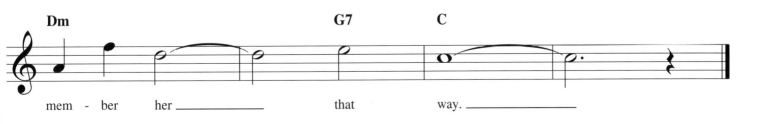

mem - ber   her _____   that   way. _____

LET'S TAKE AN OLD-FASHIONED WALK
from the Stage Production MISS LIBERTY

Words and Mus
IRVING BEF

Bright Waltz tempo

Let's   take   an   old - fash - ioned   walk. _____
Let's   take   a   stroll   through   the   park _____

_____   I'm   just   burst - ing   with   talk. _____   What   a
_____   down   a   lane   where   it's   dark _____   and   a

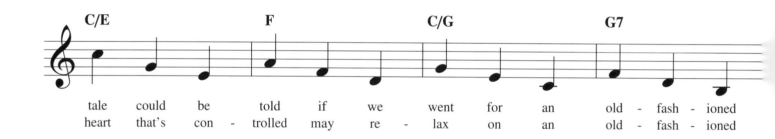

tale   could   be   told   if   we   went   for   an   old - fash - ioned
heart   that's   con - trolled   may   re - lax   on   an   old - fash - ioned

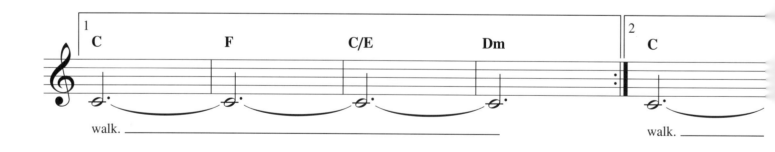

walk. _____   walk. _____

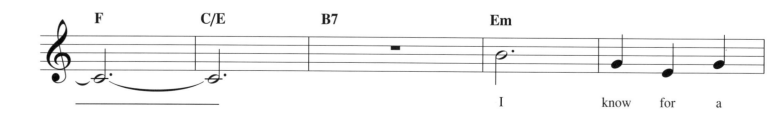

_____   I   know   for   a

couple who seem to be miles a - part, _____

____ there's noth - ing like walk - ing and hav - ing a

"heart to heart." _____ I

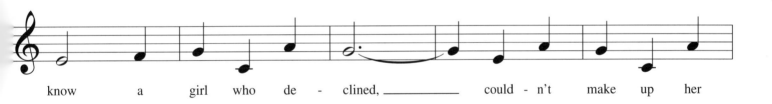

know a girl who de - clined, _____ could - n't make up her

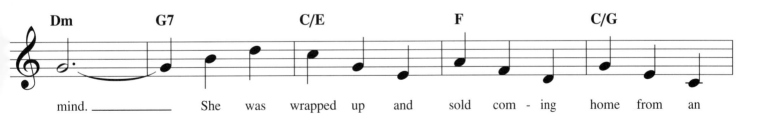

mind. _____ She was wrapped up and sold com - ing home from an

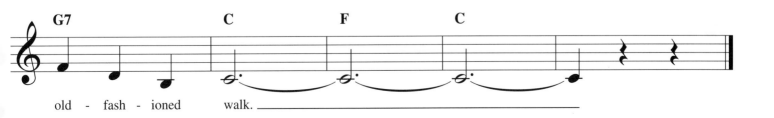

old - fash - ioned walk. _____

LILI MARLENE

Words and Music by MACK DA
HANS LEIP and NORBERT SCHU

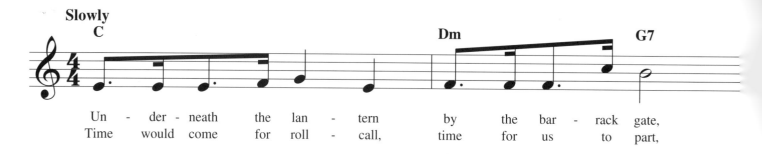

Un - der - neath the lan - tern by the bar - rack gate,
Time would come for roll - call, time for us to part,

dar - ling, I re - mem - ber the way you used to wait. 'Twas
dar - ling, I'd ca - ress you and press you to my heart. And

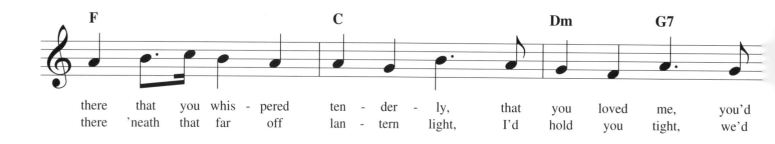

there that you whis - pered ten - der - ly, that you loved me, you'd
there 'neath that far off lan - tern light, I'd hold you tight, we'd

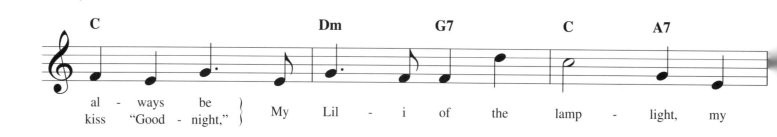

al - ways be   }
kiss "Good - night,"   } My Lil - i of the lamp - light, my

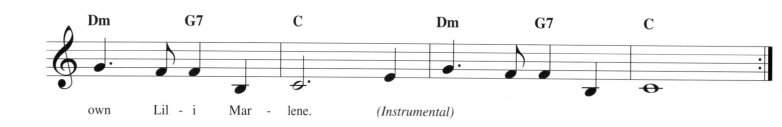

own Lil - i Mar - lene.   (Instrumental)

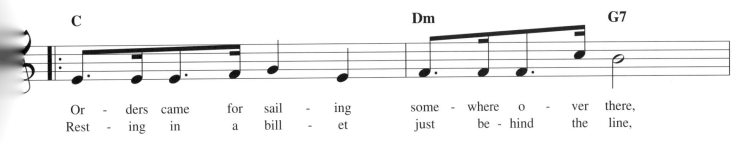

Or - ders came for sail - ing some - where o - ver there,
Rest - ing in a bill - et just be - hind the line,

all con - fined to bar - racks was more than I could bear. I
e - ven tho' we're part - ed your lips are close to mine. You

knew you were wait - ing in the street, I heard your feet, but
wait where that lan - tern soft - ly gleams, your sweet face seems to

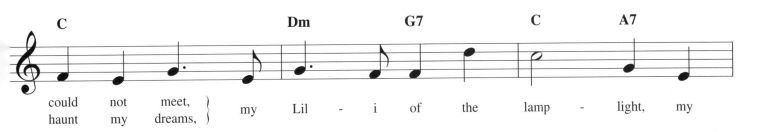

could not meet, } my Lil - i of the lamp - light, my
haunt my dreams, }

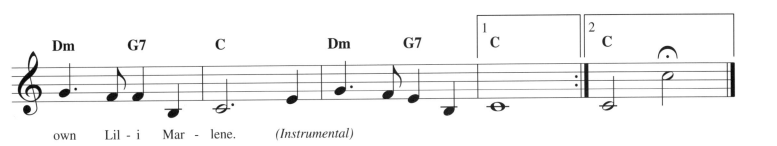

own Lil - i Mar - lene. *(Instrumental)*

109

LONG AGO (AND FAR AWAY)
from COVER GIRL

Words by IRA GERSH*
Music by JEROME KE

Moderately slow

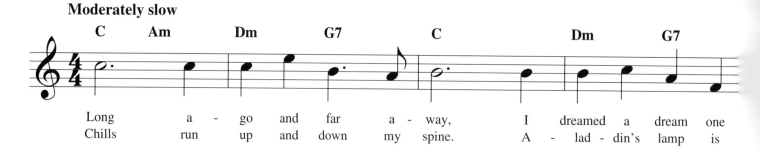

Long _____ a - go and far a - way, _____ I dreamed a dream one
Chills run up and down my spine. A - lad - din's lamp is

day, and now that dream is here be - side me.
mine. The dream I dreamed was not de - nied me.

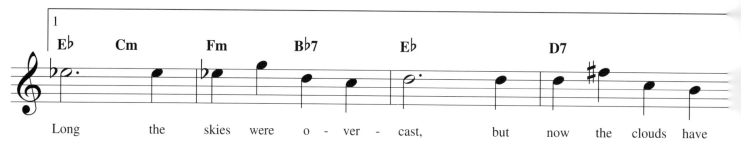

Long the skies were o - ver - cast, but now the clouds have

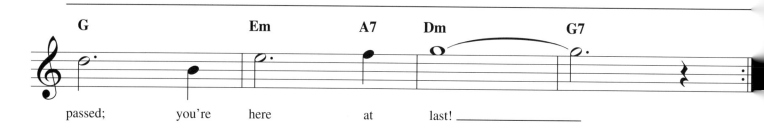

passed; you're here at last! _____

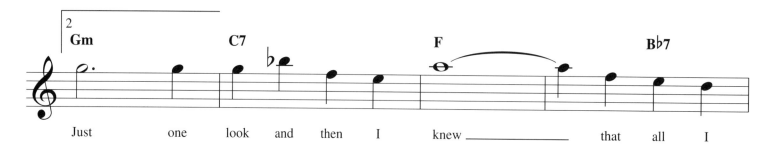

Just one look and then I knew _____ that all I

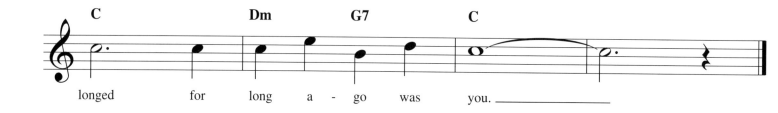

longed for long a - go was you. _____

LOVE LETTERS
Theme from the Paramount Picture LOVE LETTERS

Words by EDWARD HEYMAN
Music by VICTOR YOUNG

Gracefully

Love let - ters straight from your heart, _____ keep us so

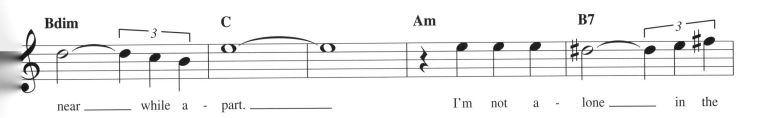

near _____ while a - part. _____ I'm not a - lone _____ in the

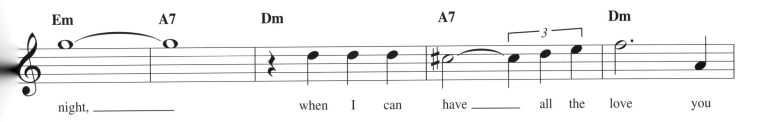

night, _____ when I can have _____ all the love you

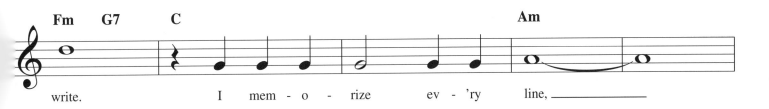

write. I mem - o - rize ev - 'ry line, _____

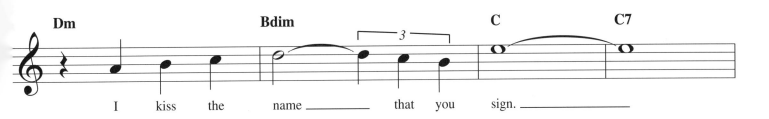

I kiss the name _____ that you sign. _____

And dar - ling, then I read a - gain right from the start

love let - ters straight from your heart. _____

LOVER MAN
(Oh, Where Can You Be?)

By JIMMY DA'
ROGER RAMIREZ and JIMMY SHERM

Blues tempo

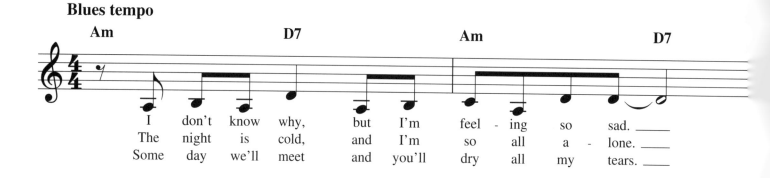

I don't know why, but I'm feel - ing so sad. _____
The night is cold, and I'm so all a - lone. _____
Some day we'll meet and you'll dry all my tears. _____

I long to try some - thing I've nev - er had. _____
I'd give my soul just to call you my own. _____
Then whis - per sweet lit - tle things in my ears. _____

Nev - er had no kiss - in', oh, what I've been miss - in'.
Got a moon a - bove me, but no one to love me.
Hug - gin' and a - kiss - in', oh, what I've been miss - in'.

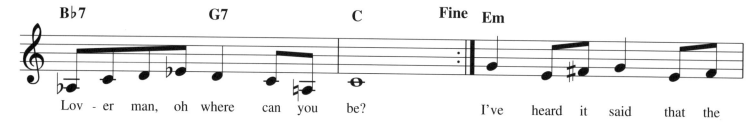

Lov - er man, oh where can you be? I've heard it said that the

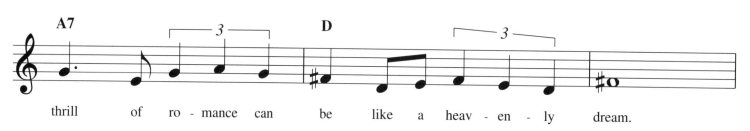

thrill of ro - mance can be like a heav - en - ly dream.

D.C. al Fine

I go to bed with a pray'r that you'll make love to me, strange as it seems.

MAÑANA

Words and Music by PEGGY LEE
and DAVE BARBOUR

MAIRZY DOATS

Words and Music by MILTON DRAKE
AL HOFFMAN and JERRY LIVINGSTON

Lightly

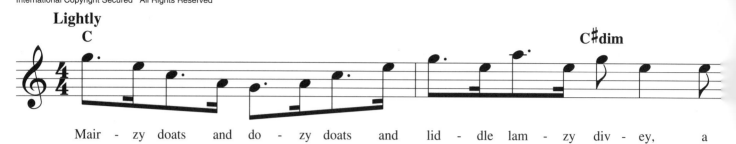

Mair - zy doats and do - zy doats and lid - dle lam - zy div - ey, a

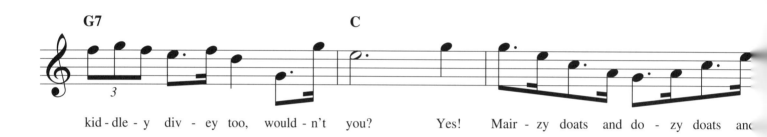

kid - dle - y div - ey too, would - n't you? Yes! Mair - zy doats and do - zy doats and

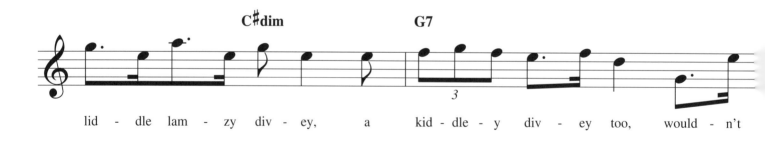

lid - dle lam - zy div - ey, a kid - dle - y div - ey too, would - n't

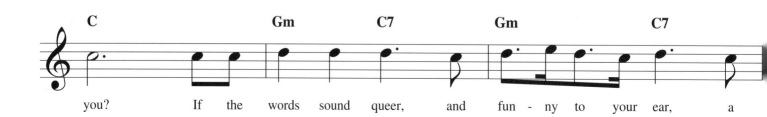

you? If the words sound queer, and fun - ny to your ear, a

lit - tle bit   jum - bled and   jiv - ey,   sing   "Mares   eat   oats   and

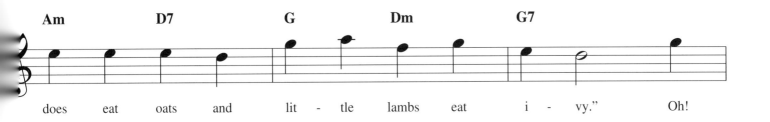

does   eat   oats   and   lit - tle   lambs   eat   i - vy."   Oh!

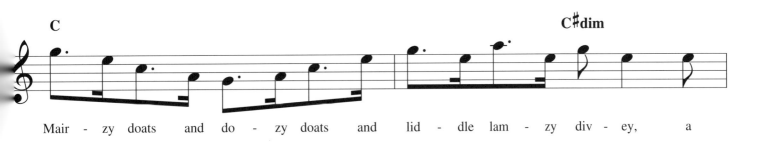

Mair - zy doats   and do - zy doats   and   lid - dle lam - zy div - ey,   a

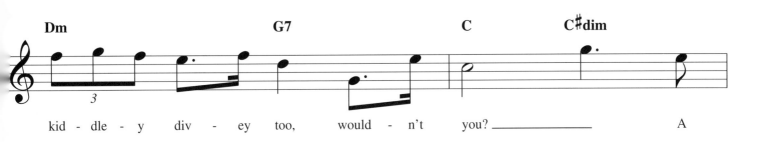

kid - dle - y div - ey too,   would - n't   you? _____   A

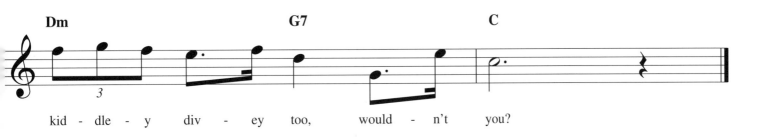

kid - dle - y div - ey too,   would - n't   you?

MOONLIGHT IN VERMONT

Words and Music by JOHN BLACKB
and KARL SUESSD

Slowly

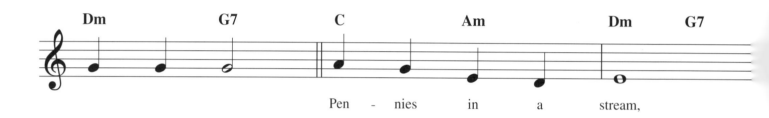

Pen - nies   in   a   stream,

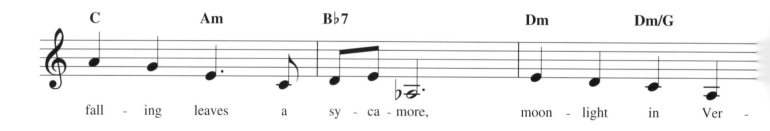

fall - ing   leaves   a   sy - ca - more,   moon - light   in   Ver -

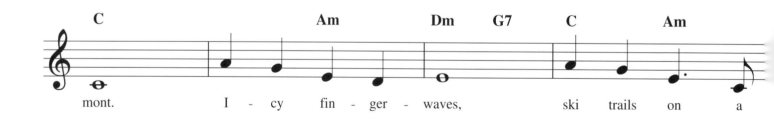

mont.   I - cy   fin - ger - waves,   ski   trails   on   a

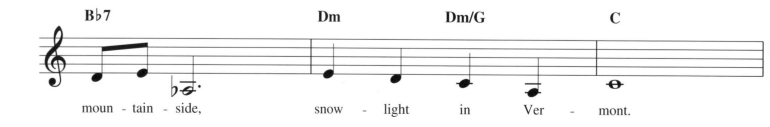

moun - tain - side,   snow - light   in   Ver - mont.

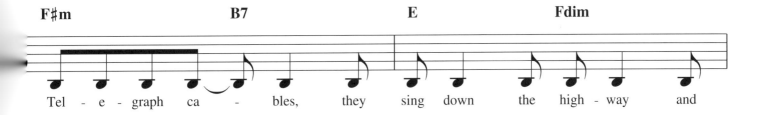

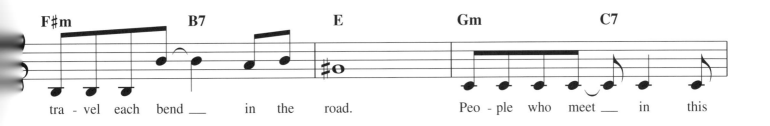

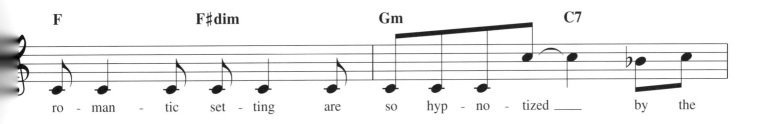

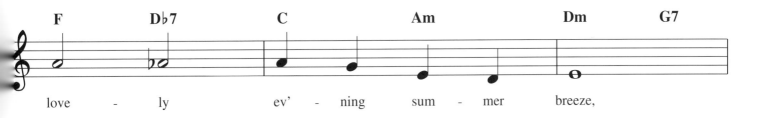

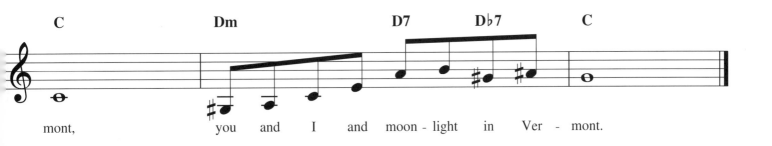

MY FOOLISH HEART
from MY FOOLISH HEART

Words by NED WASHING
Music by VICTOR YO

Slowly and expressively

The night _____ is like a love-ly tune. Be-ware _____ my fool-ish

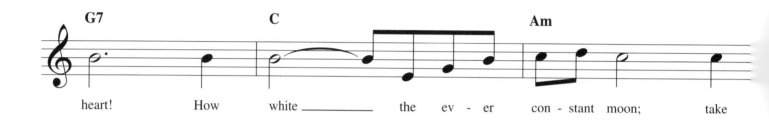

heart! How white _____ the ev-er con-stant moon; take

care _____ my fool-ish heart! There's a line be-tween love and fas-ci-

na-tion _____ that's hard to see on an eve-ning such as this. For they

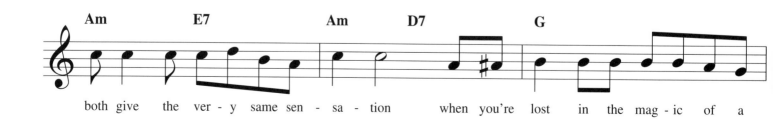

both give the ver-y same sen-sa-tion when you're lost in the mag-ic of a

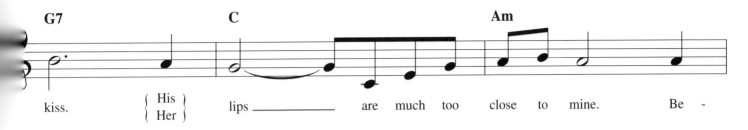

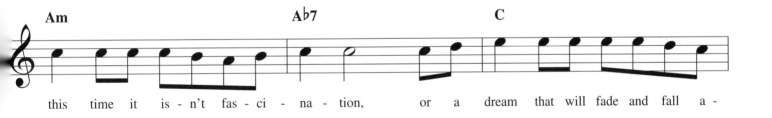

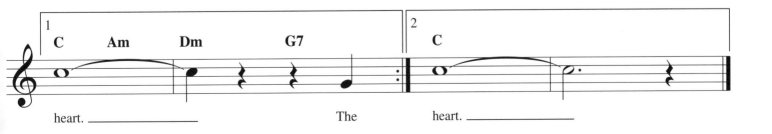

NATURE BOY

Words and Mus
EDEN AH

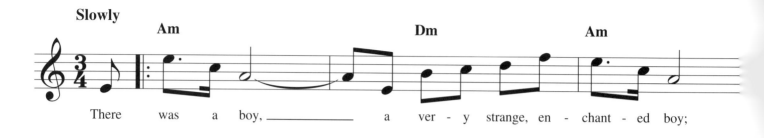

There was a boy, _____ a ver - y strange, en - chant - ed boy;

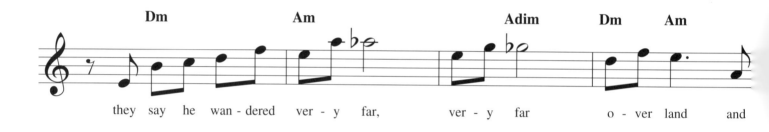

they say he wan - dered ver - y far, ver - y far o - ver land and

sea. A lit - tle shy _____ and sad of eye, _____

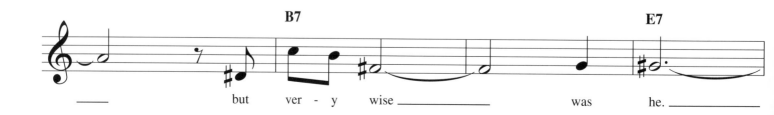

_____ but ver - y wise _____ was he. _____

And then one day, _____ one mag - ic day, he passed my way.

And as we spoke of man - y things, fools and kings, this he said to

me: "The great - est thing _____ you'll ev - er learn _____

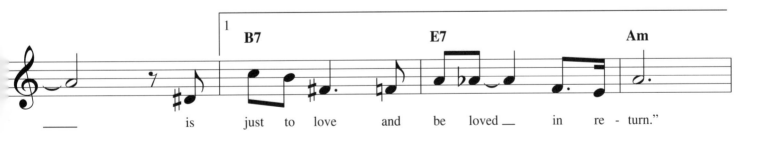

_____ is just to love and be loved __ in re - turn."

There just to love and be loved in re - turn." _____

A NIGHTINGALE SANG IN BERKELEY SQUARE

Lyric by ERIC MASCHW...
Music by MANNING SHER...

123

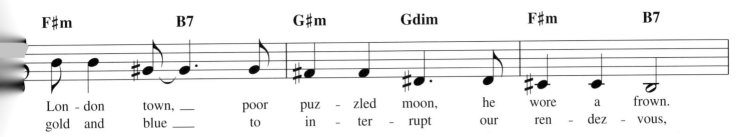

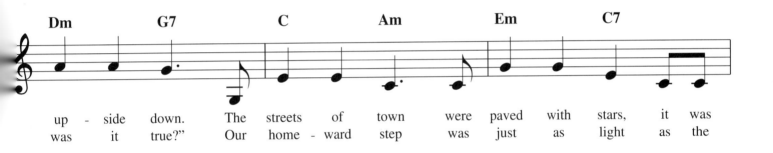

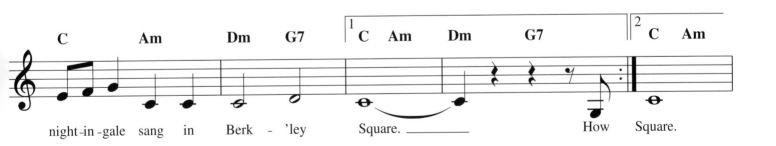

NO MOON AT ALL

By DAVE M/
and REDD EV/

With a beat

No moon at all, _____ what a night, ____
Don't make a sound, ___ it's so dark, ____

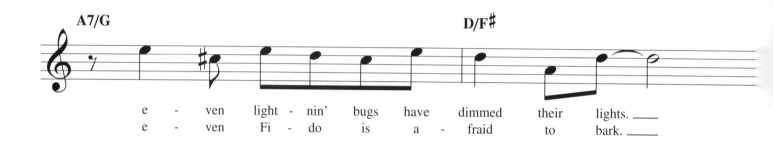

e - ven light - nin' bugs have dimmed their lights. ____
e - ven Fi - do is a - fraid to bark. ____

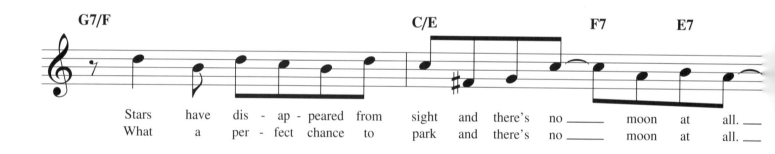

Stars have dis - ap - peared from sight and there's no ____ moon at all. __
What a per - fect chance to park and there's no ____ moon at all. __

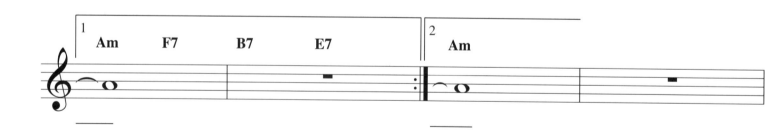

Should we want at - mos - phere, _ for in - spir - a -

- tion, dear, __ one kiss will make __ it clear, __ that to -

night is right and bright moon - light might in - ter - fere. __

No moon at all __ up a - bove. __ This is noth - ing like they

told us of. __ Just to think we fell in

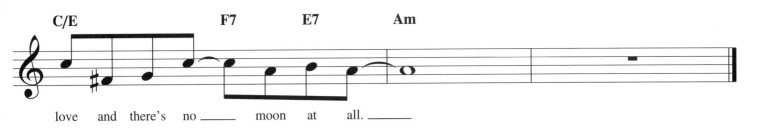

love and there's no __ moon at all. __

OLD DEVIL MOON
from FINIAN'S RAINBOW

Words by E.Y. HARBU
Music by BURTON L

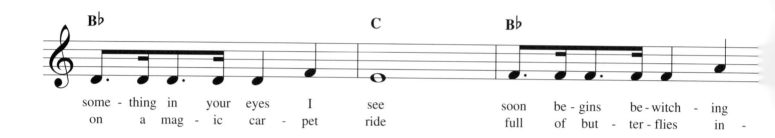

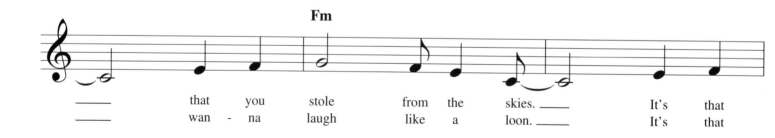

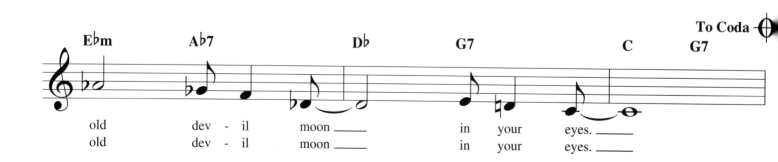

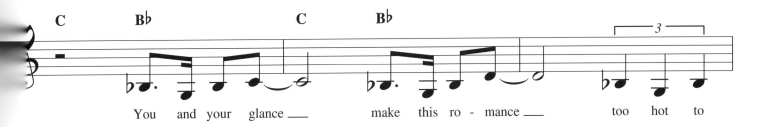

You and your glance ___ make this ro - mance ___ too hot to

han - dle. ___ Stars in the night ___ blaz - ing their light ___

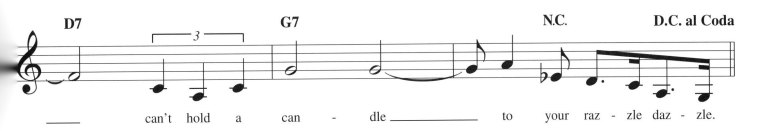

___ can't hold a can - dle ___ to your raz - zle daz - zle.

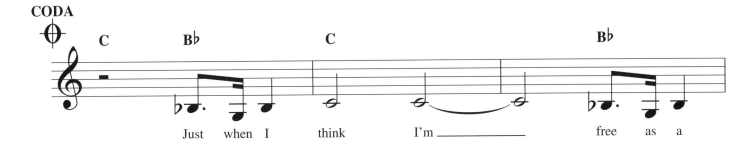

Just when I think I'm ___ free as a

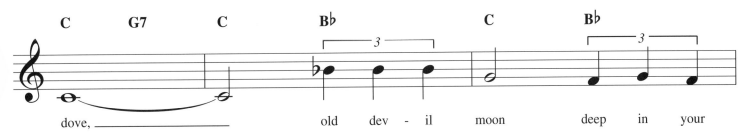

dove, ___ old dev - il moon deep in your

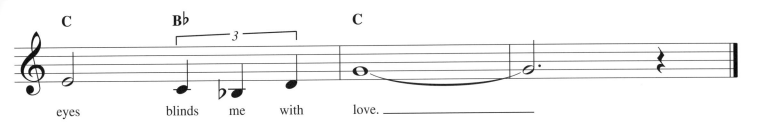

eyes blinds me with love. ___

ON A SLOW BOAT TO CHINA

By FRANK LOESS

ONE DOZEN ROSES

Words by ROGER LEWIS and "COUNTRY" JOE WASHBURN
Music by DICK JURGENS and WALTER DONOVAN

OPEN THE DOOR, RICHARD!

Words by "DUSTY" FLETCHER and JOHN MAS
Music by JACK McVEA and DAN HOW

Vigorously

O - pen the door, Rich - ard! O - pen the door and

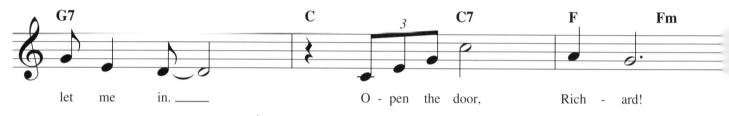

let me in. _____ O - pen the door, Rich - ard!

Rich - ard, why don't you o - pen that door? o - pen the door? I'm

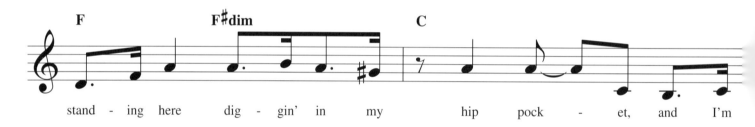

stand - ing here dig - gin' in my hip pock - et, and I'm

stand - in' here scratch - in' in my pants pock - et, and I'm

stand - ing here grop - in' in my coat pock - et, and I

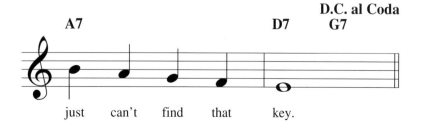

just can't find that key.

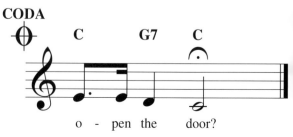

o - pen the door?

PISTOL PACKIN' MAMA

Words and Music by
AL DEXTER

Bright Country

1. Drink - in' beer in a cab - a - ret, ____ and was I hav - in'
2. She kicked out my wind - shield, ____ she hit me over the
3.-6. *(See additional lyrics)*

fun! Un - til one night she caught me right, ____ and
head. She cussed and cried, and said I'd lied, ____ and

Chorus

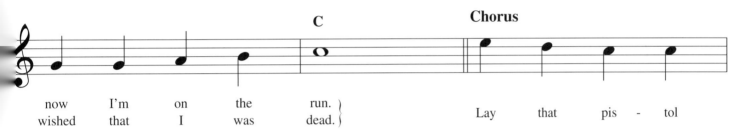

now I'm on the run.)
wished that I was dead.)   Lay that pis - tol

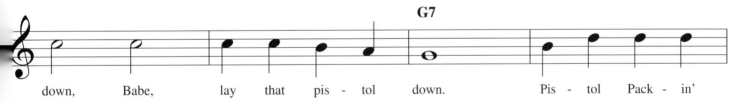

down, Babe, lay that pis - tol down. Pis - tol Pack - in'

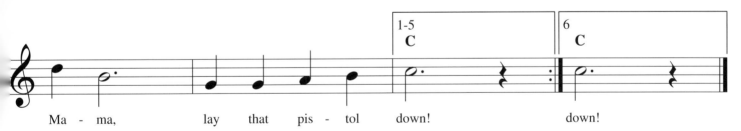

Ma - ma, lay that pis - tol down!   down!

1-5
C

6
C

Additional Lyrics

3. Drinkin' beer in a cabaret,
And dancing with a blonde,
Until one night she shot out the light,
Bang! That blonde was gone.
(To Chorus)

4. I'll see you ev'ry night, Babe,
I'll woo you ev'ry day.
I'll be your regular daddy
If you'll put that gun away.
(To Chorus)

5. Drinkin' beer in a cabaret,
And was I havin' fun!
Until one night she caught me right,
And now I'm on the run.
(To Chorus)

6. Now there was old Al Dexter,
He always had his fun,
But with some lead, she shot him dead.
His honkin' days were done…
(Chorus to last ending)

SEEMS LIKE OLD TIMES
from ARTHUR GODFREY AND HIS FRIENDS

Lyric and Music by JOHN JACOB L
and CARMEN LOMBA

Moderately

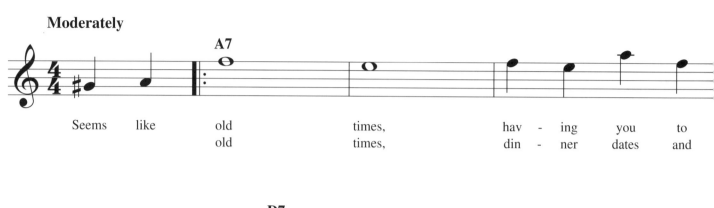

Seems like old times, hav-ing you to
old times, din-ner dates and

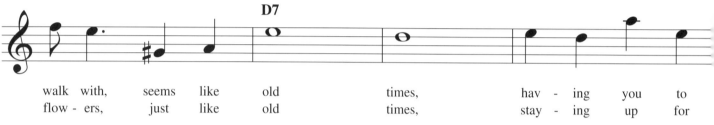

walk with, seems like old times, hav-ing you to
flow-ers, just like old times, stay-ing up for

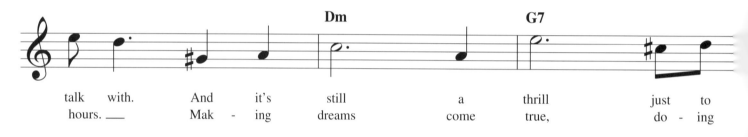

talk with. And it's still a thrill just to
hours. __ Mak-ing dreams come true, do-ing

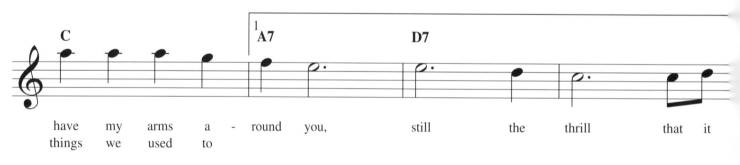

have my arms a-round you, still the thrill that it
things we used to

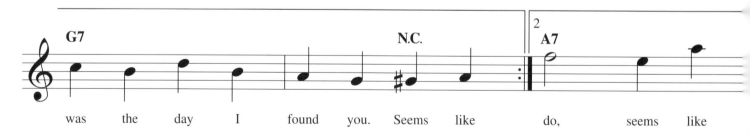

was the day I found you. Seems like do, seems like

old times, __ be-ing here with you. __

A SUNDAY KIND OF LOVE

Words and Music by BARBARA BELLE,
LOUIS PRIMA, ANITA LEONARD and STAN RHODES

SENTIMENTAL JOURNEY

Words and Music by BUD GREEN
LES BROWN and BEN HOMER

Moderately

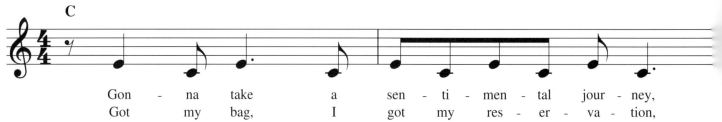

Gon - na take a sen - ti - men - tal jour - ney,
Got my bag, I got my res - er - va - tion,

gon - na set my heart at ease. _____
spent each dime I could af - ford. _____

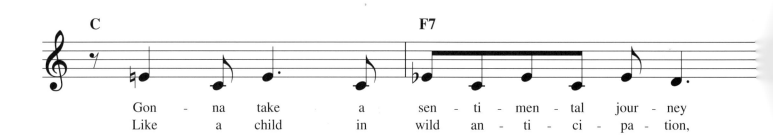

Gon - na take a sen - ti - men - tal jour - ney
Like a child in wild an - ti - ci - pa - tion,

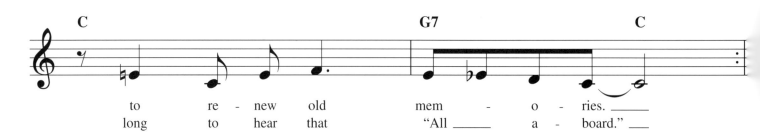

to re - new old mem - o - ries. _____
long to hear that "All _____ a - board." _____

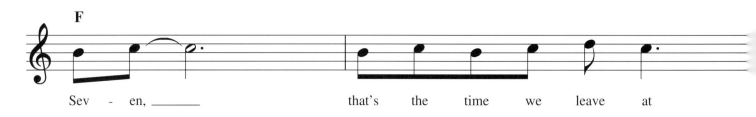

Sev - en, _____ that's the time we leave at

sev - en, _____ I'll be wait - in' up for

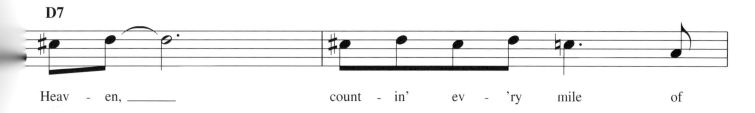

Heav - en, _____ count - in' ev - 'ry mile of

rail - road track _____ that takes me back. _____

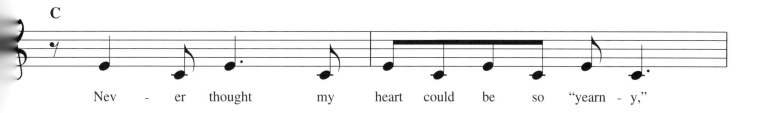

Nev - er thought my heart could be so "yearn - y,"

why did I de - cide to roam? ____

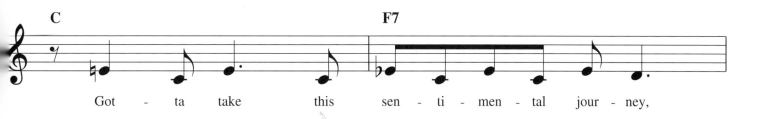

Got - ta take this sen - ti - men - tal jour - ney,

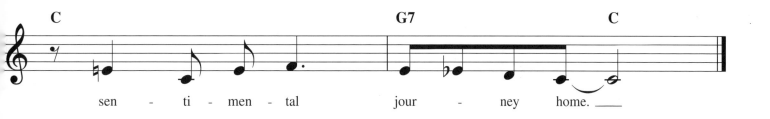

sen - ti - men - tal jour - ney home. _____

SENTIMENTAL ME

Words by JIMMY CAS
Music by JIM MOREH

Moderately

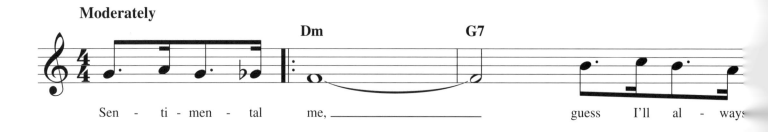

Sen - ti - men - tal me, _____ guess I'll al - ways

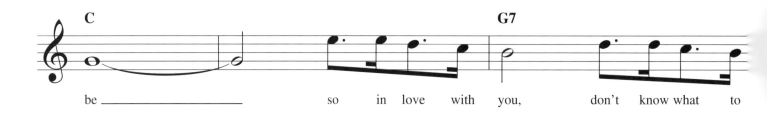

be _____ so in love with you, don't know what to

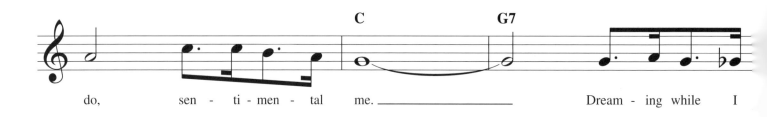

do, sen - ti - men - tal me. _____ Dream - ing while I

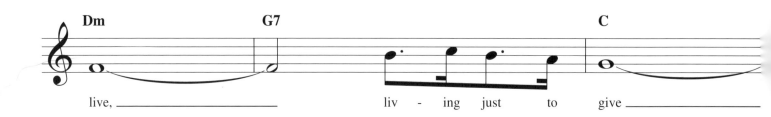

live, _____ liv - ing just to give _____

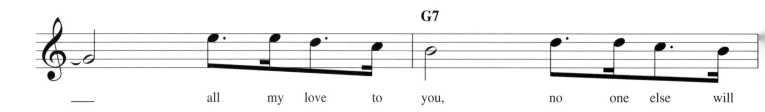

____ all my love to you, no one else will

SLEEPY LAGOON

Words by JACK LAWRENCE
Music by ERIC COATES

A sleep - y la - goon, a trop - i - cal

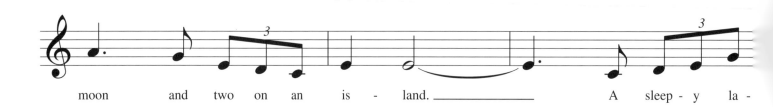

moon and two on an is - land. A sleep - y la -

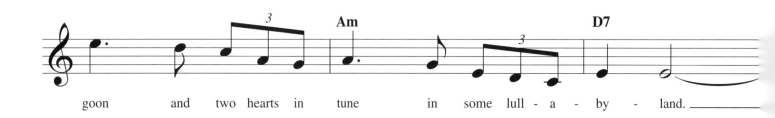

goon and two hearts in tune in some lull - a - by - land.

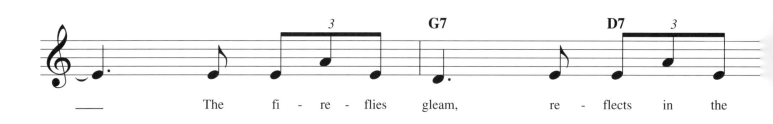

The fi - re - flies gleam, re - flects in the

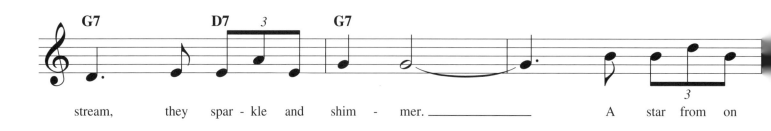

stream, they spar - kle and shim - mer. A star from on

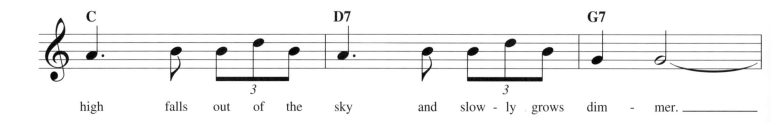

high falls out of the sky and slow - ly grows dim - mer.

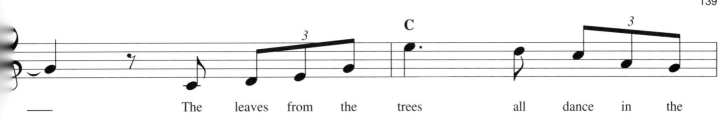

The leaves from the trees all dance in the

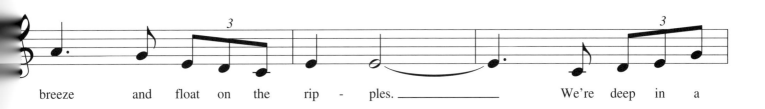

breeze and float on the rip - ples. _____ We're deep in a

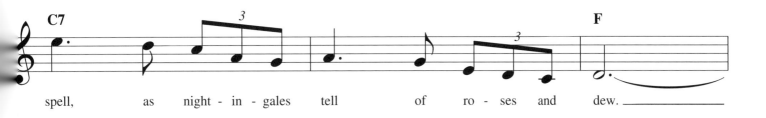

spell, as night - in - gales tell of ro - ses and dew. _____

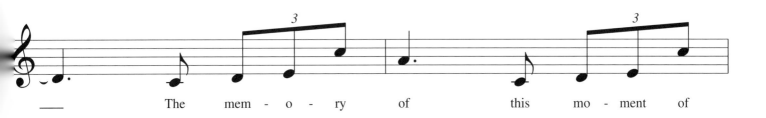

_____ The mem - o - ry of this mo - ment of

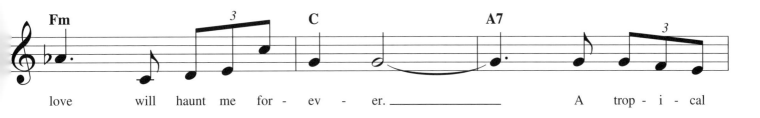

love will haunt me for - ev - er. _____ A trop - i - cal

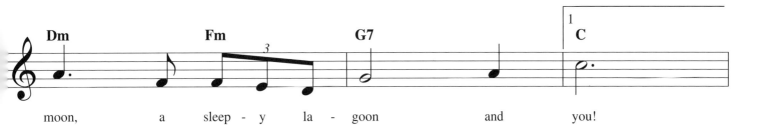

moon, a sleep - y la - goon and you!

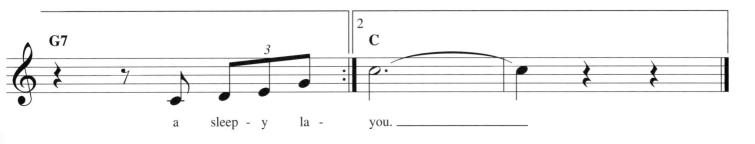

a sleep - y la - you. _____

STELLA BY STARLIGHT
from the Paramount Picture THE UNINVITED

Words by NED WASHINGTON
Music by VICTOR YOUNG

Moderately

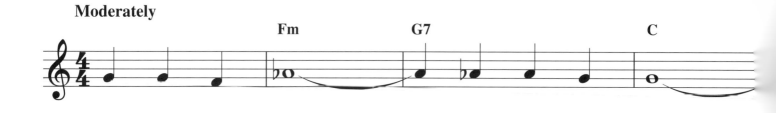

The song _____ a rob - in sings _____ through

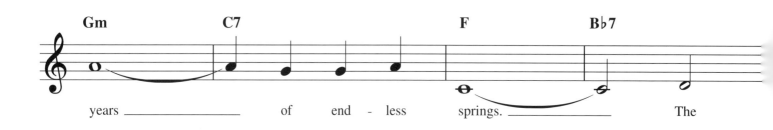

years _____ of end - less springs. _____ The

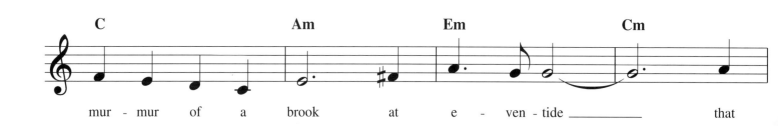

mur - mur of a brook at e - ven - tide _____ that

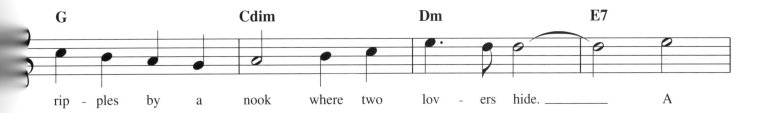

rip - ples by a nook where two lov - ers hide. _____ A

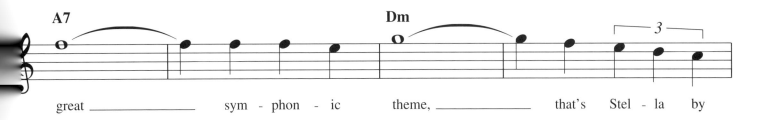

great _____ sym - phon - ic theme, _____ that's Stel - la by

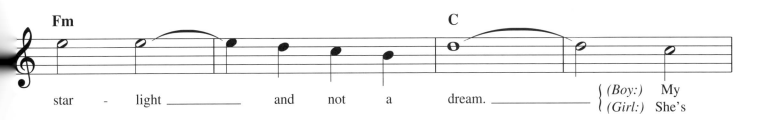

star - light _____ and not a dream. _____ { (Boy:) My / (Girl:) She's

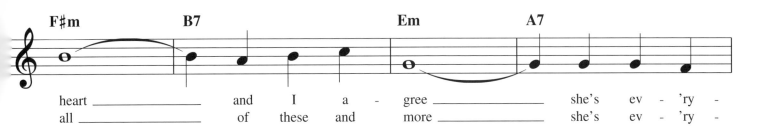

heart _____ and I a - gree _____ she's ev - 'ry -
all _____ of these and more _____ she's ev - 'ry -

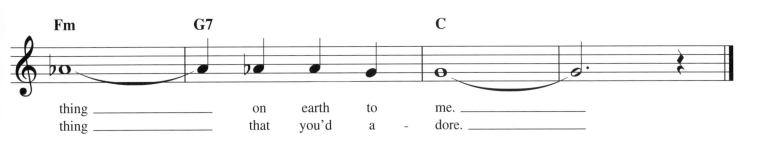

thing _____ on earth to me. _____
thing _____ that you'd a - dore. _____

THE SURREY WITH THE FRINGE ON TOP
from OKLAHOMA!

Lyrics by OSCAR HAMMERSTE
Music by RICHARD RODGE

With a lilt

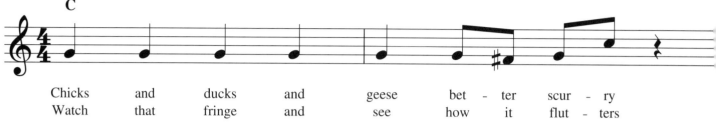

Chicks and ducks and geese bet - ter scur - ry
Watch that fringe and see how it flut - ters

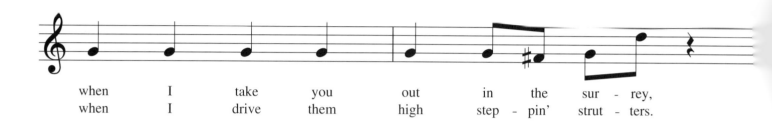

when I take you out in the sur - rey,
when I drive them out high step - pin' strut - ters.

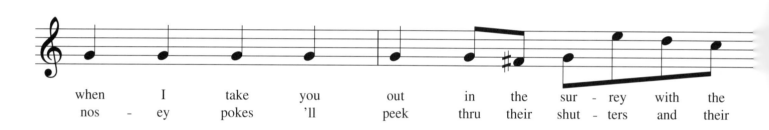

when I take you out in the sur - rey with the
nos - ey pokes 'll peek thru their shut - ters and their

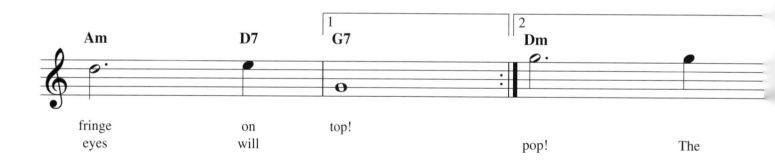

fringe on top!
eyes will pop! The

wheels are yel - ler, the up - hol - ster - y's brown, the

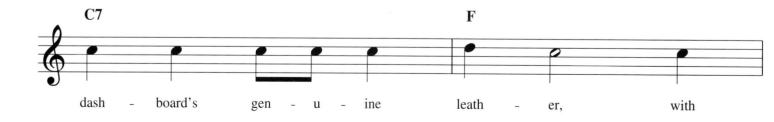

dash - board's gen - u - ine leath - er, with

143

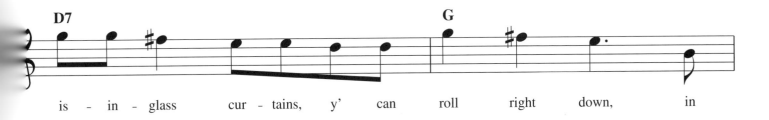

is - in - glass cur - tains, y' can roll right down, in

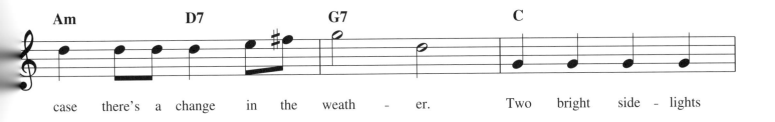

case there's a change in the weath - er. Two bright side - lights

wink - in' and blink - in', ain't no fin - er

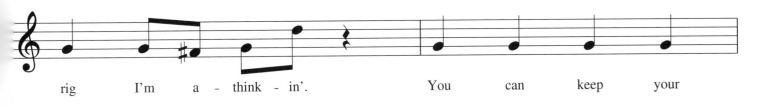

rig I'm a - think - in'. You can keep your

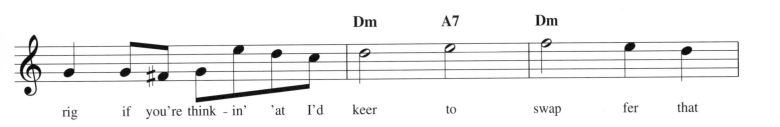

rig if you're think - in' 'at I'd keer to swap fer that

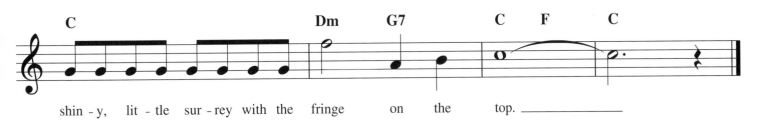

shin - y, lit - tle sur - rey with the fringe on the top. ____

TANGERINE
from the Paramount Picture THE FLEET'S IN

Words by JOHNNY MERC
Music by VICTOR SCHERTZING

Medium Swing

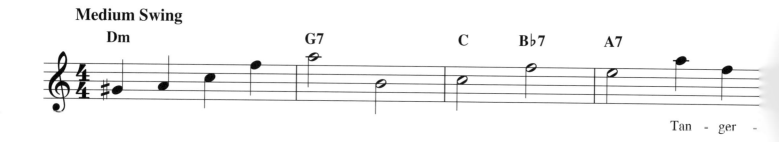

Tan - ger -

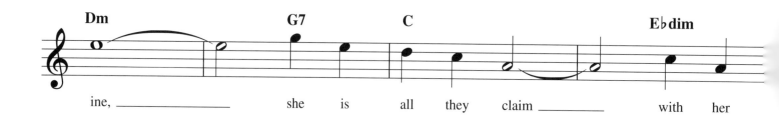

ine, _____ she is all they claim _____ with her

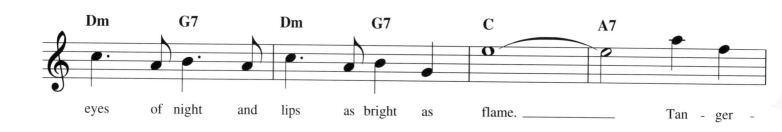

eyes of night and lips as bright as flame. _____ Tan - ger -

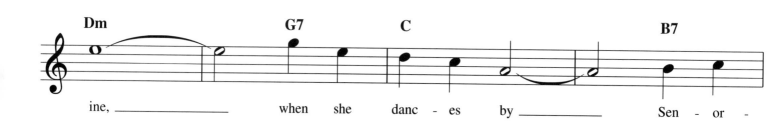

ine, _____ when she danc - es by _____ Sen - or -

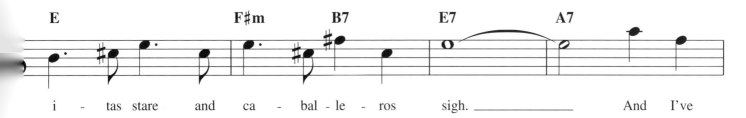

i - tas stare and ca - bal - le - ros sigh. _____ And I've

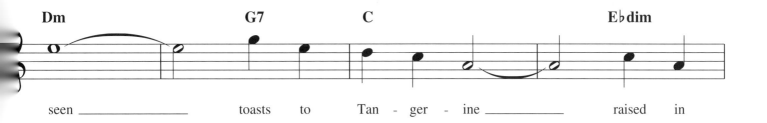

seen _____ toasts to Tan - ger - ine _____ raised in

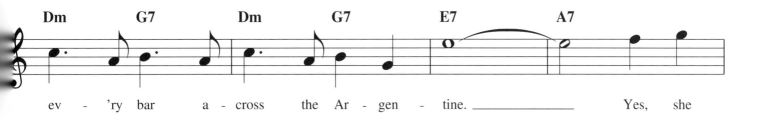

ev - 'ry bar a - cross the Ar - gen - tine. _____ Yes, she

has them all on the run but her heart be - longs to just one. Her

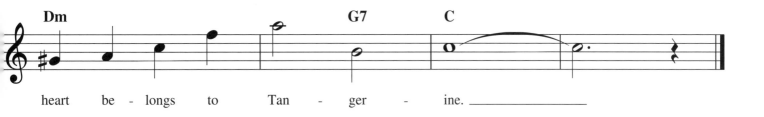

heart be - longs to Tan - ger - ine. _____

TENDERLY
from TORCH SONG

Lyric by JACK LAWRE
Music by WALTER GR

Moderately

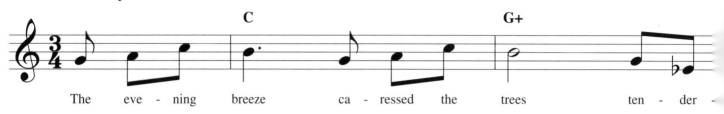

The eve - ning breeze ca - ressed the trees tender -

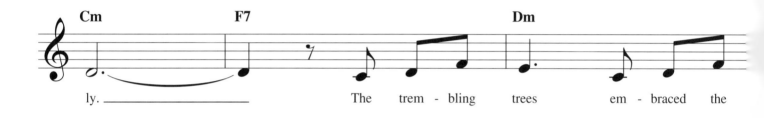

ly. _____ The trem - bling trees em - braced the

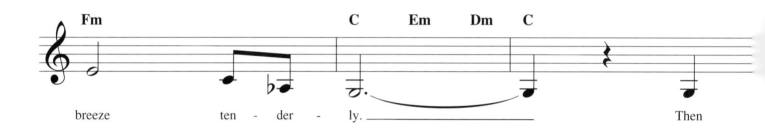

breeze ten - der - ly. _____ Then

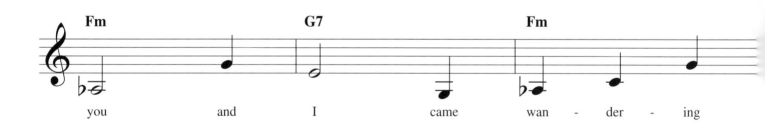

you and I came wan - der - ing

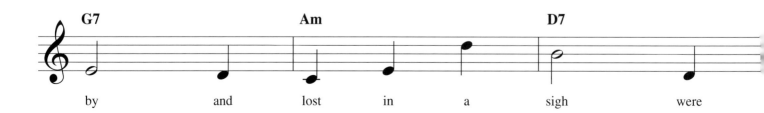

by and lost in a sigh were

we. _____ The shore was kissed by sea and

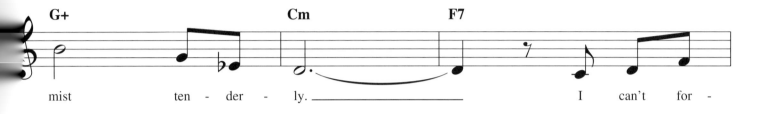

mist ten - der - ly. _____ I can't for -

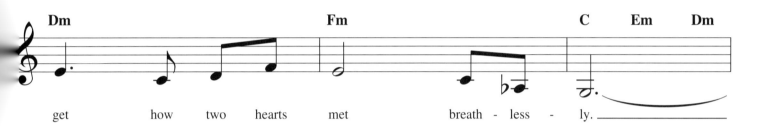

get how two hearts met breath - less - ly. _____

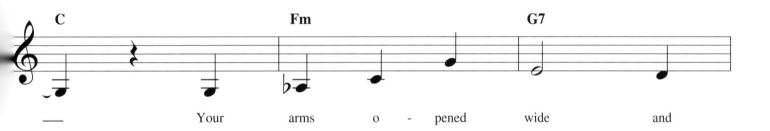

___ Your arms o - pened wide and

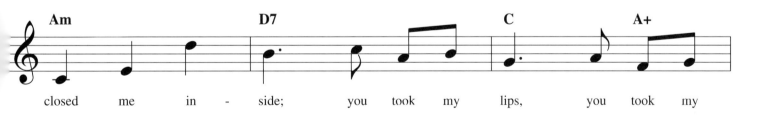

closed me in - side; you took my lips, you took my

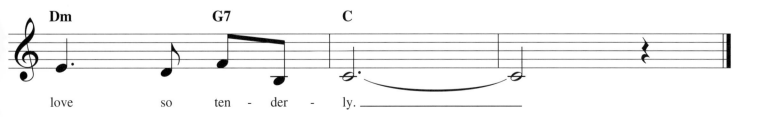

love so ten - der - ly. _____

THAT OLD BLACK MAGIC
from the Paramount Picture STAR SPANGLED RHYTHM

Words by JOHNNY MER(
Music by HAROLD AR

THEY SAY IT'S WONDERFUL
from the Stage Production ANNIE GET YOUR GUN

Words and Music
IRVING BER

Slowly

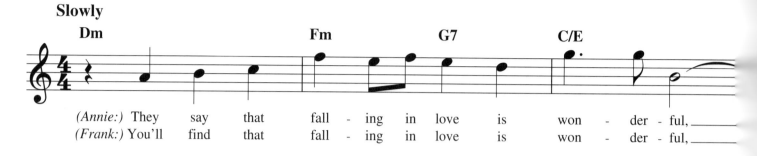

(Annie:) They say that fall - ing in love is won - der - ful, _____
(Frank:) You'll find that fall - ing in love is won - der - ful, _____

_____ it's won - der - ful _____ so they
_____ it's won - der - ful _____ *(Annie:)* so you

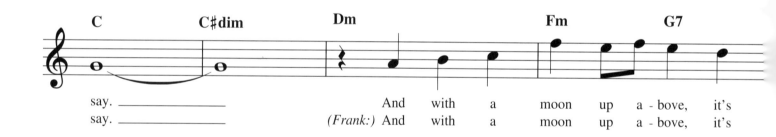

say. _____ And with a moon up a - bove, it's
say. _____ *(Frank:)* And with a moon up a - bove, it's

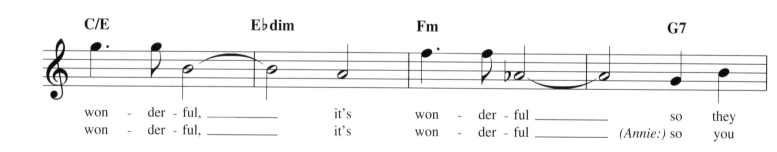

won - der - ful, _____ it's won - der - ful _____ so they
won - der - ful, _____ it's won - der - ful _____ *(Annie:)* so you

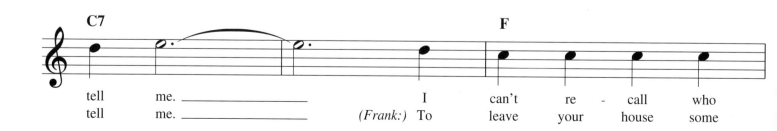

tell me. _____ I can't re - call who
tell me. _____ *(Frank:)* To leave your house some

said it, I know I nev - er read it, I
morn - ing, and with - out an - y warn - ing, you're

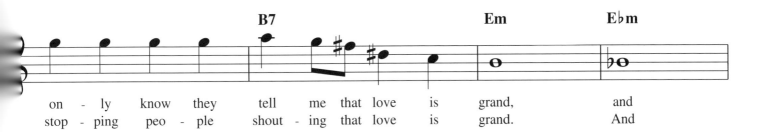

on - ly know they tell me that love is grand, and
stop - ping peo - ple shout - ing that love is grand. And

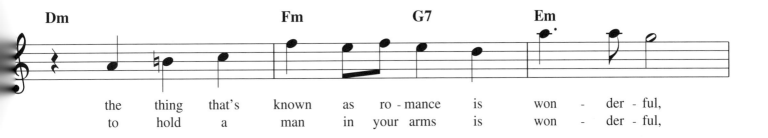

the thing that's known as ro - mance is won - der - ful,
to hold a man in your arms is won - der - ful,

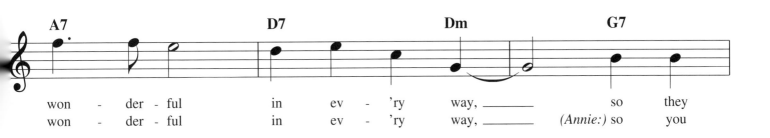

won - der - ful in ev - 'ry way, _____ so they
won - der - ful in ev - 'ry way, _____ (Annie:) so you

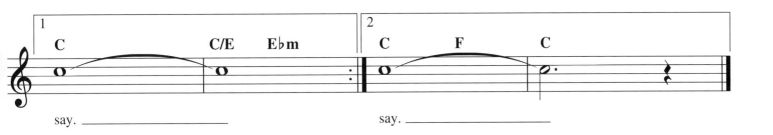

say. _____   say. _____

THE THINGS WE DID LAST SUMMER

Words by SAMMY C
Music by JULE ST

The boat rides we would take, the moon-light on the lake, the

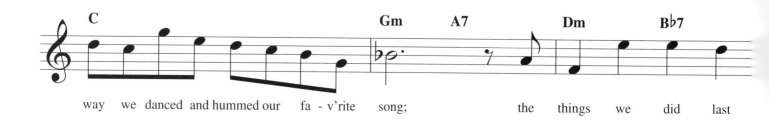

way we danced and hummed our fa-v'rite song; the things we did last

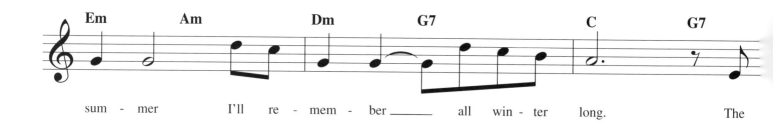

sum-mer I'll re-mem-ber all win-ter long. The

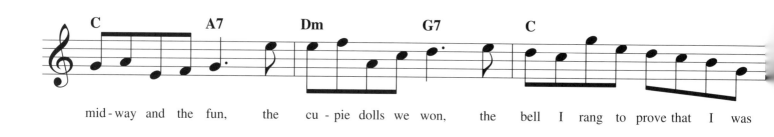

mid-way and the fun, the cu-pie dolls we won, the bell I rang to prove that I was

strong; the things we did last sum-mer I'll re-

mem - ber _____ all win - ter long. The ear - ly morn - ing hike, the

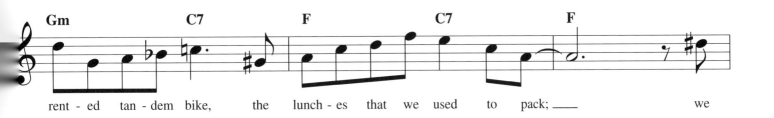

rent - ed tan - dem bike, the lunch - es that we used to pack; _____ we

nev - er could ex - plain that sud - den sum - mer rain, the looks we got when we got back. _

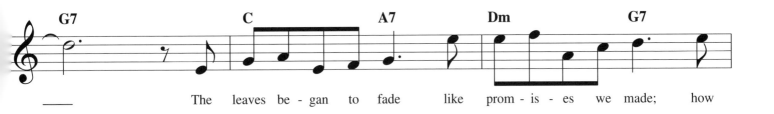

_____ The leaves be - gan to fade like prom - is - es we made; how

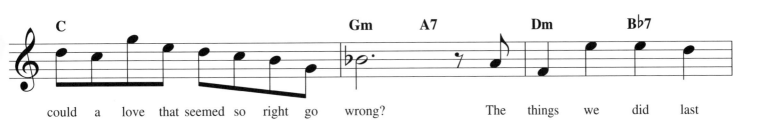

could a love that seemed so right go wrong? The things we did last

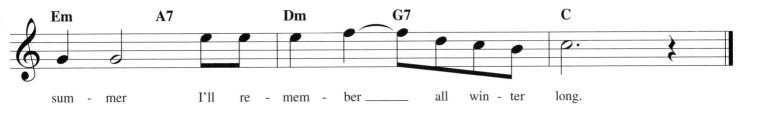

sum - mer I'll re - mem - ber _____ all win - ter long.

(THERE'LL BE BLUEBIRDS OVER) THE WHITE CLIFFS OF DOVER

Words by NAT BURT
Music by WALTER KE

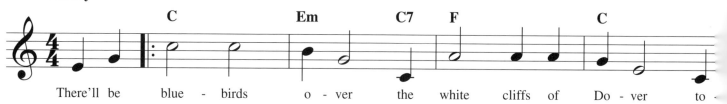

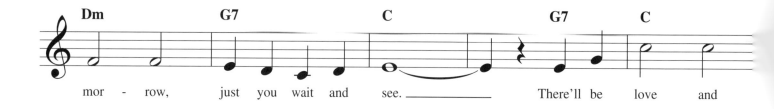

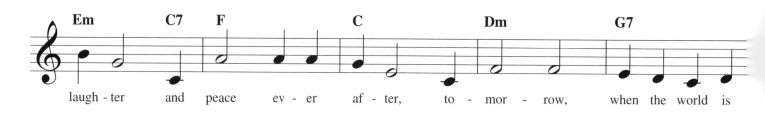

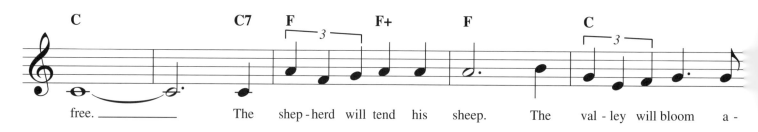

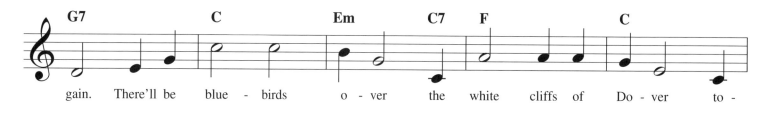

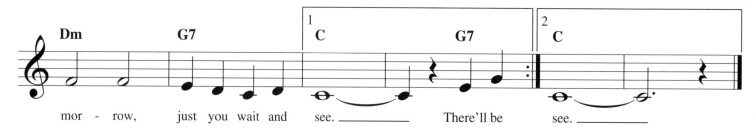

YOU ALWAYS HURT THE ONE YOU LOVE

Words and Music by ALLAN ROBERTS
and DORIS FISHER

Moderately

You al - ways hurt the one you love, the one you should-n't

hurt at all. _____ You al - ways take the sweet - est

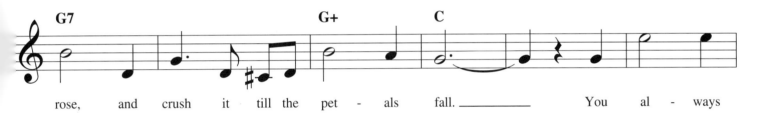

rose, and crush it till the pet - als fall. _____ You al - ways

break the kind - est heart, with a hast - y word you can't re - call. _____

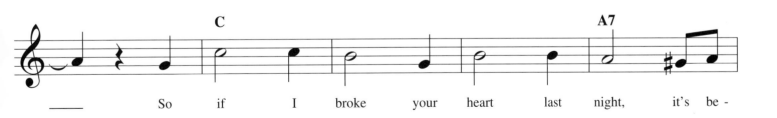

_____ So if I broke your heart last night, it's be -

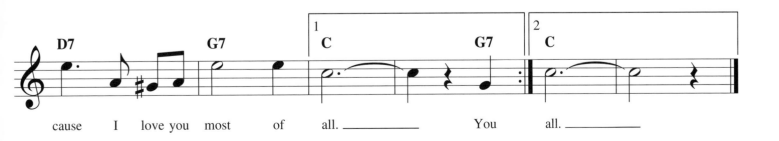

cause I love you most of all. _____ You all. _____

WHY DON'T YOU DO RIGHT
(Get Me Some Money, Too!)

By JOE McC

You had plen - ty mon - ey nine - teen twen - 'y two, ___ you

let oth - er peo - ple make a fool of you. ___ Why don't you do right, ___

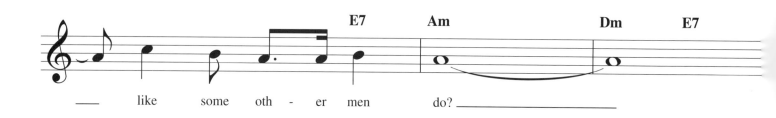

___ like some oth - er men do? ___

Get out of here and get me some mon - ey too. ___

___ Yo' sit - tin' down ___ won - d'ring what it's all a - bout, ___ if you

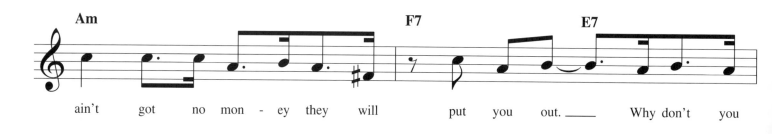

ain't got no mon - ey they will put you out. ___ Why don't you

do right, _____ like some oth - er men do? _____

Get out of here and get me some mon - ey too. _____ If

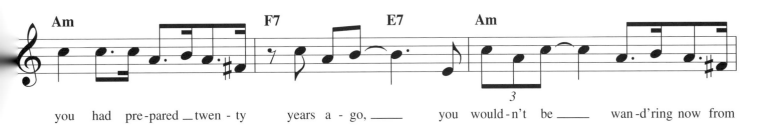

you had pre-pared _ twen - ty years a - go, _____ you would-n't be _____ wan-d'ring now from

do' to do'. _ Why don't you do right, _____ like some oth - er men do? _____

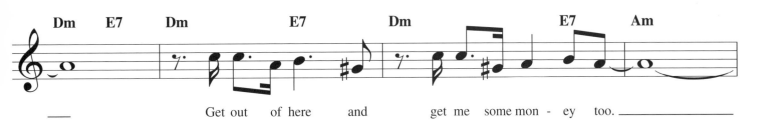

_____ Get out of here and get me some mon - ey too. _____

_____ Why don't you do right _____ like some oth - er men do, _

_____ like some oth - er men do. _____

A WONDERFUL GUY
from SOUTH PACIFIC

Lyrics by OSCAR HAMMERSTEIN
Music by RICHARD RODGERS

Moderately bright

I'm as corn - y as Kan - sas in Au - gust,
I am in a con - ven - tion - al dith - er,

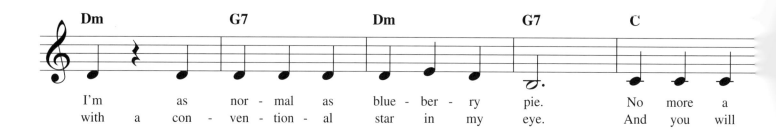

I'm as nor - mal as blue - ber - ry pie. No more a
with a con - ven - tion - al star in my eye. And you will

smart lit - tle girl with no heart, I have found me a
note there's a lump in my throat when I speak of that

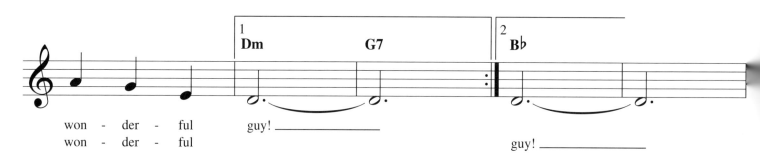

won - der - ful guy! _____
won - der - ful guy! _____

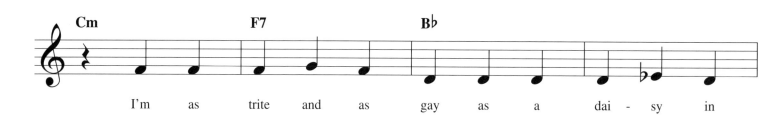

I'm as trite and as gay as a dai - sy in

May, a cli - ché com - ing true! _____

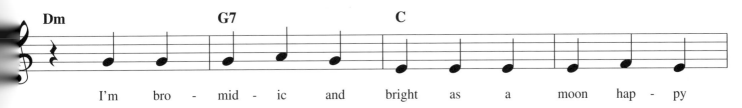

I'm bro - mid - ic and bright as a moon hap - py

night pour - ing light on the dew! _____

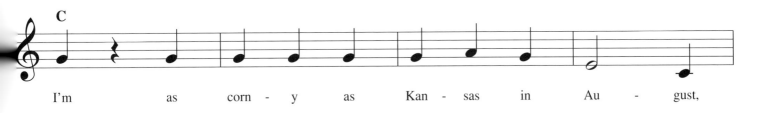

I'm as corn - y as Kan - sas in Au - gust,

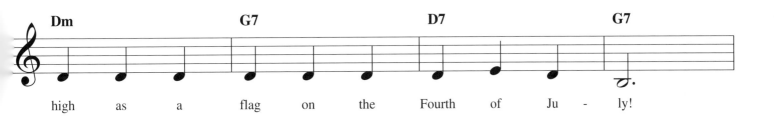

high as a flag on the Fourth of Ju - ly!

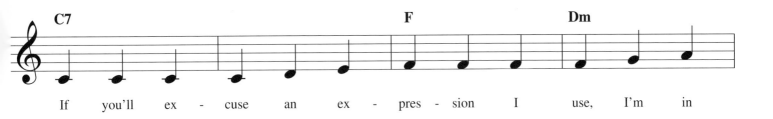

If you'll ex - cuse an ex - pres - sion I use, I'm in

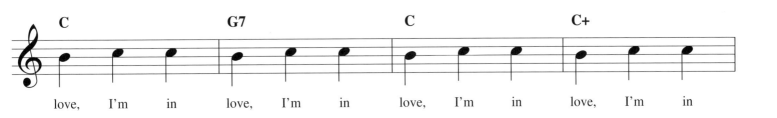

love, I'm in love, I'm in love, I'm in love, I'm in

love with a won - der - ful guy! _____

WUNDERBAR
from KISS ME, KATE

Words and Music
COLE PORTER

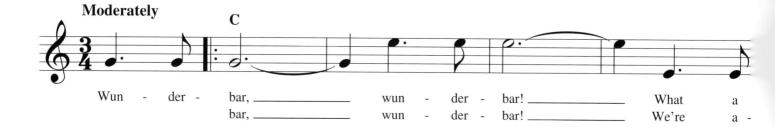

Wun - der - bar, _____ wun - der - bar! _____ What a
bar, _____ wun - der - bar! _____ We're a -

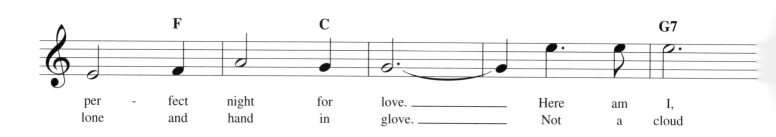

per - fect night for love. _____ Here am I,
lone and hand in glove. _____ Not a cloud

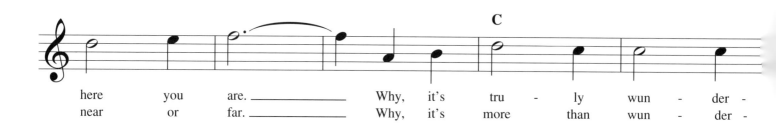

here you are. _____ Why, it's tru - ly wun - der -
near or far. _____ Why, it's more than wun - der -

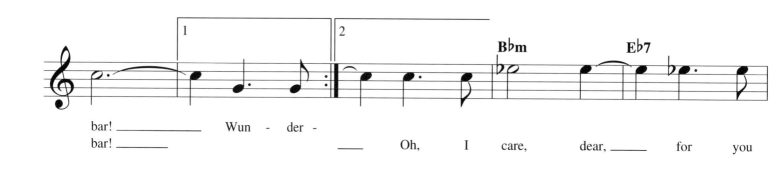

bar! _____ Wun - der -
bar! _____ Oh, I care, dear, _____ for you

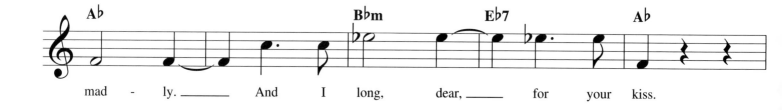

mad - ly. _____ And I long, dear, _____ for your kiss.

I would die, dear, _____ for you glad - ly. _____ You're di -

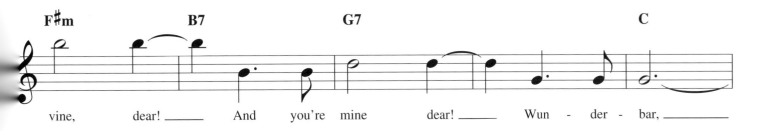

vine, dear! _____ And you're mine dear! _____ Wun - der - bar, _____

_____ wun - der - bar! _____ There's our fa - v'rite star a -

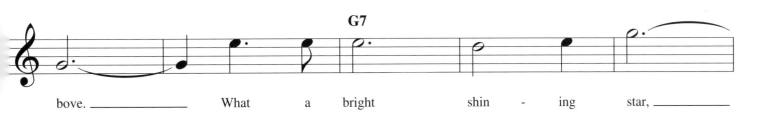

bove. _____ What a bright shin - ing star, _____

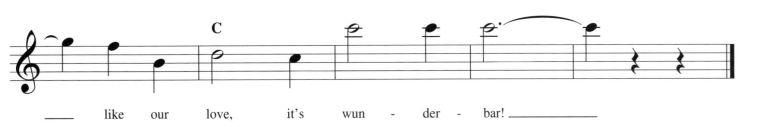

_____ like our love, it's wun - der - bar! _____

YOU DON'T KNOW WHAT LOVE IS

Words and Music by DON R.
and GENE DE P.

Slowly

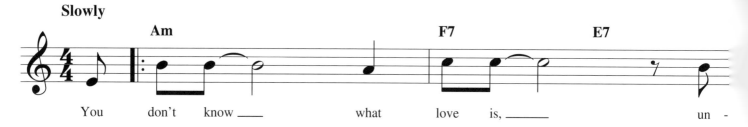

You   don't   know ___   what   love   is, ___   un -

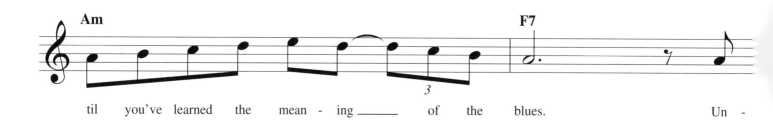

til   you've   learned   the   mean - ing ___   of   the   blues.   Un -

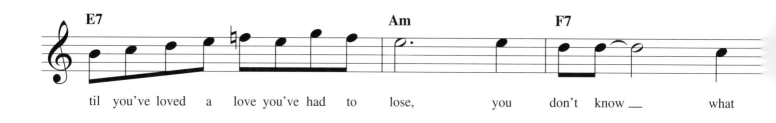

til   you've   loved   a   love   you've   had   to   lose,   you   don't   know ___   what

love   is. ___   You   don't   know ___   how   lips   hurt, ___   un -

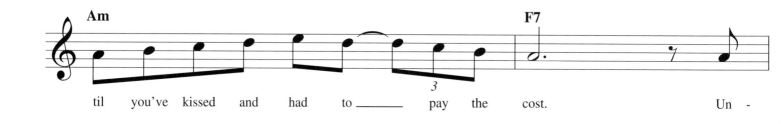

til   you've   kissed   and   had   to ___   pay   the   cost.   Un -

YOU'D BE SO NICE TO COME HOME TO
from SOMETHING TO SHOUT ABOUT

Words and Mus
COLE POR

Moderately

You'd be so nice to come home to, _____ you'd be
so nice _____ by the fire. _____ While the breeze on
high _____ sang a lull - a - by, _____ you'd be all that
I could de - sire. _____ Un - der stars, chilled _____ by the
win - ter, _____ un - der an Au - gust moon, burn - ing a -
bove. _____ You'd be so nice, you'd be par - a -
dise to come home to _____ and love. _____

YOU'RE NOBODY 'TIL SOMEBODY LOVES YOU
featured in the Broadway Musical CONTACT

Words and Music by RUSS MORGAN,
LARRY STOCK and JAMES CAVANAUGH

YOUNGER THAN SPRINGTIME
from SOUTH PACIFIC

Lyrics by OSCAR HAMMERSTE
Music by RICHARD RODG

Moderately

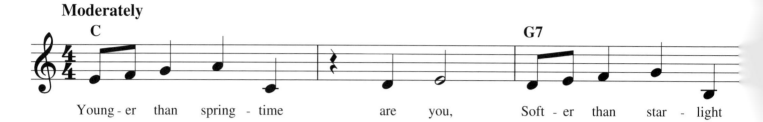

Young - er than spring - time   are   you,   Soft - er than star - light

are   you,   Warm - er than winds   of   June   are   the   gen - tle

lips   you   gave   me.   Gay - er than laugh - ter   are   you,

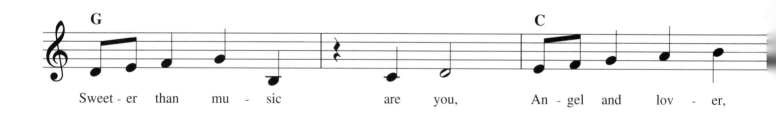

Sweet - er than mu - sic   are   you,   An - gel and lov - er,

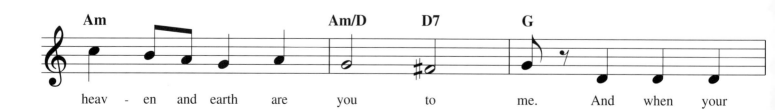

heav - en and earth   are   you   to   me.   And when your

youth and joy in - vade my arms And fill my

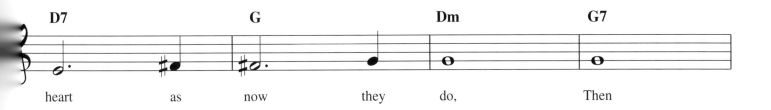

heart as now they do, Then

young - er than spring - time am I, Gay - er than laugh - ter

am I, An - gel and lov - er, heav - en and earth am

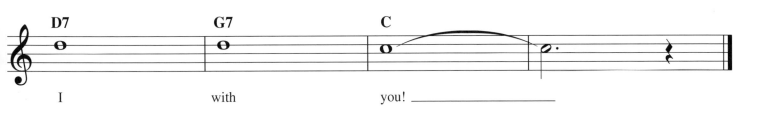

I with you! _____

CHORD SPELLER

C chords

C	C–E–G
Cm	C–Eb–G
C7	C–E–G–Bb
Cdim	C–Eb–Gb
C+	C–E–G#

C# or Db chords

C#	C#–F–G#
C#m	C#–E–G#
C#7	C#–F–G#–B
C#dim	C#–E–G
C#+	C#–F–A

D chords

D	D–F#–A
Dm	D–F–A
D7	D–F#–A–C
Ddim	D–F–Ab
D+	D–F#–A#

Eb chords

Eb	Eb–G–Bb
Ebm	Eb–Gb–Bb
Eb7	Eb–G–Bb–Db
Ebdim	Eb–Gb–A
Eb+	Eb–G–B

E chords

E	E–G#–B
Em	E–G–B
E7	E–G#–B–D
Edim	E–G–Bb
E+	E–G#–C

F chords

F	F–A–C
Fm	F–Ab–C
F7	F–A–C–Eb
Fdim	F–Ab–B
F+	F–A–C#

F# or Gb chords

F#	F#–A#–C#
F#m	F#–A–C#
F#7	F#–A#–C#–E
F#dim	F#–A–C
F#+	F#–A#–D

G chords

G	G–B–D
Gm	G–Bb–D
G7	G–B–D–F
Gdim	G–Bb–Db
G+	G–B–D#

G# or Ab chords

Ab	Ab–C–Eb
Abm	Ab–B–Eb
Ab7	Ab–C–Eb–Gb
Abdim	Ab–B–D
Ab+	Ab–C–E

A chords

A	A–C#–E
Am	A–C–E
A7	A–C#–E–G
Adim	A–C–Eb
A+	A–C#–F

Bb chords

Bb	Bb–D–F
Bbm	Bb–Db–F
Bb7	Bb–D–F–Ab
Bbdim	Bb–Db–E
Bb+	Bb–D–F#

B chords

B	B–D#–F#
Bm	B–D–F#
B7	B–D#–F#–A
Bdim	B–D–F
B+	B–D#–G

Important Note: A slash chord (C/E, G/B) tells you that a certain bass note is to be played under a particular harmony. In the case of C/E, the chord is C and the bass note is E.